when love lasts

forever

WHEN LOVE LASTS FOREVER

WHEN LOVE LASTS FOREVER

WHEN LOVE LASTS FOREVER

WHEN LOVE

LASTS FOREVER

WHEN LOVE LASTS FOREVER

WHEN LOVE LASTS FOREVER

WHEN LOVE LASTS FOREVER

male couples celebrate commitment

EDITED BY MERLE JAMES YOST

the pilgrim press
cleveland, ohio

when love lasts
forever

The Pilgrim Press, Cleveland, Ohio 44115

© 1999 by Merle James Yost

All rights reserved. Published 1999

Printed in Hong Kong on acid-free paper

04 03 02 01 00 99   5 4 3 2 1

Library of Congress Cataloging-in-Publication Data

Yost, Merle James, 1958–

When love lasts forever : male couples celebrate commitment / edited by Merle James Yost.

p.   cm.

ISBN 0-8298-1332-2 (alk. paper)

1. Gay male couples—United States—Biography.   2. Love—United States.

3. Same-sex marriage—United States.   I. Title.

HQ75.7.Y67   1999

306.76'62'092273—dc21   98-50331

CIP

To Reber

and the life we have created

and

to Ray and Dave

who held our hands and lit the path.

WHEN LOVE LASTS FOREVER

WHEN LOVE LASTS FOREVER

WHEN LOVE LASTS FOREVER

WHEN LOVE

LASTS FOREVER

WHEN LOVE LASTS FOREVER

WHEN LOVE LASTS FOREVER

WHEN LOVE LASTS FOREVER

contents

CONTENTS

preface

My partner, Frank Reber Brown, and I have been together for over fifteen years. When we coupled, we only knew one other male couple at the time, and they introduced us. This was before unions were in and courtship was considered a normal part of the process. Ray and Dave took us under their wing and helped us to lay a solid foundation for a future together. They allowed us to see the difficult parts of being together in addition to the joy. My hope for this book is that it will be the mentor for other male couples that Ray and Dave were for us.

Because of our longevity as a couple, like so many others, we have found ourselves role models for some gay men. Because of the nature of gay couples, it has been difficult to find other couples with which to socialize. I believe that when we spend time with others we are more grateful for our joys and less critical of our sorrows. By the time this book is published we will have been together for sixteen years. It is hard to remember a time pre-Reber. We have both changed dramatically since that first meeting, and in the next sixteen years we will change a great deal more. As far as I am concerned, that is the promise and excitement of a long-term relationship.

Hopefully, the stories in this book will show another generation that coupling is possible. As a therapist, I have seen many men come into my office and tell me that they do not believe that gay men are capable of getting into relationships and staying in them. They have bought the public perception that gay men are only interested in sex. This belief about men in general and gay men in particular has done untold harm to our self-perception as men and to our ability to form relationships. This book refutes this myth by showing that men have coupled for a very long time and continue to do so.

My second hope for this book is that it will be a support for couples that are often isolated from other male couples. We have a tendency to mate, to move to the suburbs, to buy a house, and to never be heard from again unless we break up and go back on the market. This book is to remind gay couples that there are others in similar relationships and that we all have problems. Each couple finds its own compromises and solutions to the problems that face it. One person who read the manuscript said that after the first two or three stories she forgot that it was about gay couples and simply understood the universality of being in a couple and the sorrows and joys that accompany the journey.

Another reason for editing this book is that it might help the families, friends, and even enemies of gays understand that our relationships are rather ordinary. There is far more to being gay than sex, just as there is far more to being straight than sex. Our lives are complex, layered with families, friends, and jobs. We have kids, survive accidents, face insecurities, and make tough decisions. But like any couple, our love and commitment to each other is what sees us through. Yes, we also have differences because we are two men in a relationship. The good part is that we have less socialization about what it means to be in a relationship. The bad part is that we often try to apply heterosexual programming to our relationships anyway.

When the germ of an idea for this book began, I thought that writing it would take a few months and that it would be effortless. Having cowritten three other books that each took an average of about three months to write, I was completely unprepared for the difficulty of completing this anthology and getting it published. However, it has been a labor of love, and I have enjoyed corresponding with so many wonderful couples.

This collection of stories includes a wide range of writing styles and writing abilities. I made a conscious choice not to alter the stories. Who these people are as a couple is revealed both through the stories they have written and in the way they have written them. There is a wide range in the educational level of the contributors, several of whom have been published before. Most of my editing has come in the form of suggestions about what is covered rather than how it is covered.

This is not and has no pretensions of being a literary anthology. My own writing does not fall into a literary category, and I have neither the skill nor interest in producing such a book. I have tried to produce an anthology that is readable and most of all accessible. The emotion and content of the stories are my primary consideration.

Probably the most difficult and controversial part of the book has been my insistence on using the real names and pictures of the couples. Many people decided not to contribute after I made it clear that this was a condition for inclusion. The pictures and real names are a clear signal to demonstrate our pride and joy in our relationships. Not using the real names and pictures might have suggested that we are ashamed or embarrassed in some way. In my communication with all of these couples, I have been delighted to find men who celebrate their lives and relationships and who are willing to share them with the world.

In many ways, the pictures are as important as the stories in conveying information about gay couples. Each story is accompanied by two pictures of the couple—one from the beginning of their relationship and another more recent photograph. In contrast to a popular gay culture that values the packaging over the package, these pictures are a reminder that the body changes and that couples must value the person inside the body when marrying. Physical beauty does not equal mental health, compatibility, or future attractiveness. As external physical features fade or change, there has to be something more that attracts men to each other if the relationship is to survive. These pictures are a reminder of our mortality and that we can and do grow old together. That is the goal and the joy of being in a long-term relationship.

At the same time, I have been saddened by the amount of internalized homophobia I observed in some of the long-term couples that I encountered. It is understandable that when men who coupled fifteen, twenty, or even forty years ago found someone of a like mind, they then formed a partnership that locked out the rest of the world because developing a gay identity is a relatively recent phenomenon. Because they have been part of a couple, partners in these long-term relationships have not had the opportunity to experience themselves as part of the larger (gay) community and develop a sense of (gay) self. Instead, in many cases they are paired with someone who reinforces their prejudices about what it means to be gay or homosexual. Since they have separated themselves from the gay community, their projections and beliefs have never been challenged.

The majority of the couples that contributed to the book are involved in the larger community as well as the gay community. Because the reflection of others like and different from ourselves is crucial to our evolving identity and sense of self, those who have found a connection to the community are generally healthier because of it.

Couples are the best and worst of people. Couples exemplify what love and support can do for people, and we also see how coupling can isolate and reinforce the worst of our negative self-beliefs and actions. All of the relationships in this book are of significant length, and they show the difficulties experienced by any two people getting together to share their lives and the problems that come with that choice over a long period of time.

I have made every effort to be inclusive in this anthology. I have actively sought stories from around the world, from as many ethnic and cultural groups as I could locate, from all religions, and from subcultures within the gay community. I am proud of the diversity in the anthology.

No discussion of gay couples can ignore the issue of AIDS. This disease has impacted every couple in some way. One of my goals has been to record and measure that impact. Even the longest-term couple, two men who have been together for forty-five years, has had to deal with AIDS. I am thankful that the contributors have shared with us their pain and fears concerning AIDS. As we learn from these stories, being in a couple is not a complete shelter from AIDS.

I am grateful to everyone who has taken the time to write his story and send it to me. I have tried to pick the best and feel that the stories here represent gay couples everywhere. I hope that this anthology is a comfort for many and the beginning of awareness for others. As we take pride in our lives and reveal ourselves, we will change the world.

ACKNOWLEDGMENTS

There are many people who have contributed to this anthology. First of all, I wish to thank the authors who have so generously shared their lives and love with us. Their courage and honesty are an inspiration for the next generation. Their wisdom is universal and timeless.

I would also like to thank all of the couples who shared their stories with me. I wish that I could have put all of them into this book. Every story that I received touched me in some way, and I hope that the writing of the story was useful to them in their journey as a couple.

I greatly appreciate the friends who reviewed the manuscript and gave me some badly needed perspective. They include Mark Marion and Thomas Kelem, both colleagues; Debbie Burchard, a long-time friend and supporter; Bruce Hyland, my coauthor of three books; and Carianne Galik and Eric Elkin, who are my partner's colleagues and who both contributed especially to my understanding of how this book might be viewed. I would also like to thank Terry Colbert for his generosity of time and energy for this project. He read the manuscript and added valuable insights. He also helped a few of the contributors with their writings. I will always remember his kindness and support.

A special thanks to Reber, my partner of nearly sixteen years, who has supported me in all of my projects and endeavors. He has provided me with the foundation to try time and again. Without him, I believe that I would not have accomplished so much. He is my computer expert, personal editor, biggest fan, and the love of my life. I cannot and do not wish to imagine life without him.

This book would not have been made without the efforts of both my literary agent, Sheryl Fullerton, and my acquisitions editor at Pilgrim Press, Timothy Staveteig. Both have been supportive of my ideas and energy. Their excitement and enthusiasm have been wonderful.

Finally, I want to acknowledge the courage of Pilgrim Press to publish this book. The proposal went through many hands before it found Timothy's. He clearly shared my vision of the book and who might benefit from its publication. I am heartened by the mission of Pilgrim Press to give voice to those who otherwise might not be heard.

when love lasts

forever

Kevin Paulson

and Brian Turner

- o n e -

virtue enough for miss grrrrl

KEVIN THADDEUS PAULSON

Come over for dinner Thursday night. I'll make the family lasagna," said my cousin Kitty, named after the character on *Gunsmoke*.

"Irish women should never attempt lasagna, Kitty. Stick with corned beef and cabbage."

"Lasagna. Be here at seven."

"You only make lasagna when you're trying to fix me up with someone."

"And bring some wine."

Resolutely single at the time, I spent my weekdays selling china at Macy's and my weekends in bars in Greenwich Village or out on Fire Island. As bachelorette no. 1, I did not have much use for family then, except for my cousin Kitty, who worked in the theater and therefore had access to Broadway show tickets.

Brian danced on Broadway, as a "chorus girl," eight shows a week, in the musical *La Cage aux Folles*. He hung out with the glitterati of Manhattan, the avant garde chorus gypsies and the deviant garde stage crew, one of whom was Kitty. She took one look at Brian and saw gorgeous: thin but muscular, with fine dark hair and deep brown eyes. She took a second look and saw gay, which made the Irish yenta think of me.

1

Kitty believes family is about sharing food. Still single at thirty-eight, she has a hope chest of china for eight and matching Waterford crystal. Early in my relationship with Brian, she taught us that it didn't matter how bad the food was, as long as it was served up with love. And matching china.

That night, she did indeed cook lasagna, the ancient Toal family recipe that consists of alternating layers of Ronzoni noodles held together by cottage cheese and Ragu tomato sauce. Brian nibbled at the corners of the burnt starch. I mouthed my way dutifully through the viscous goo. (A child of the sixties, I was influenced by *Romper Room*. And although I may have been more of a Don't Bee than a Do Bee, I was a faithful member of the Clean Plate Club.)

Brian had finally pushed the pasta around on the plate enough times that it looked somewhat eaten. After we walked out the door, he said, "Would you like to hit Ray's Pizza on the way to the PATH station?" Sometime over a double cheese with mushroom, we discovered our mutual fascination with *Star Trek* reruns at midnight. He got to the question first, "Your television or mine?"

"I have a black-and-white," I admitted.

"I have a nineteen-inch and color," he replied.

"I'd go a long way for nineteen inches."

"As far as Jersey City?"

A week later, I moved in. That was thirteen years ago. Brian and I are now a legend in our part of the gay community, the dancer and the deputy or, as Kitty calls us, the oldest living gay couple; our honeymoon was a cruise for two on the Ark. For almost a decade we cohabited in Jersey City, a town of no charm other than cheap rent. The apartment, above Spinocchio's funeral parlor, had three bedrooms, no insulation, and a continually changing roster of roommates. Brian and I staked out the big corner bedroom, the one with the waterbed, and we kept it for seven years before we moved to San Francisco. In those years, we made a family.

Family is not about sex or legal certificates or children. The only children we'll ever have are our Pekingeses: Miss Grrrrl, Wolfcub, and Diva, who insist upon being mentioned in this story. Our family is about our circle of ex-lovers and former roommates and fag hags and people Brian goes to modern dance concerts with because he knows I can't stand modern dance. It's about playing the same numbers in the lottery for thirteen years because if you stay together long enough you're going to win. It's about knowing exactly which issues of *The X Men* I want for my birthday. It's about all of the people who have ever shared our Christmas tree. Family is about matching china, in-laws, and a lighthouse in New England.

In September 1987, Brian and I had a commitment ceremony. We wanted to let the rest of the world know what we already knew: that we would always be important to each other. (We waited two years so that people didn't think that we *had* to get married.) We rented a bar in Chelsea, with old wooden counters, brass rails, and exposed brick, and we filled the place with white roses. Kitty insisted on her role as old maid of honor, and Miss Grrrrl acted as flower dog, peacefully chewing a bouquet of calla lilies. Neither of our parents agreed to come, so Brian and I gave each other away. And took each other back. About fifty of our friends showed up, many straight, and none had ever been to a gay wedding before. But they came, my cousin Kitty said, because no matter how strange a "gay commitment ceremony" seemed, they knew it was right for the two of us to celebrate our life together. We began the rite in darkness, then Kitty lit a candle, which flame she passed on to another and another, until the little bar glowed in the light of the family we had gathered as witness. A real priest accepted our vows that "like the circle of the rings, we will always turn toward each other." Kitty read from *The Little Prince*: "It is the time you have spent on your rose . . ." Miss Grrrrl barked when we kissed. We went off to a honeymoon in Provincetown.

In the thirteen years we've been together, Brian has put up with more than his fair share of Toal family reunions. I come from a shanty Irish Brooklyn family with no manners and less taste. Brian has choked down Vat 69 Scotch with my widowed Aunt Beatrice while Aunt Mamie mutilated turkeys, the uncles all watched football on the television, and the child cousins sneaked cans of Rheingold beer out to the stoop. Brian has coped with his in-laws by learning how to play pinochle and nibble such inhospitable dishes as sauerbraten, beef stew, and heavenly hash.

My acceptance by the matriarchy of Brian's family was not so simple. The Turner family is from Maine, and Downeaster pride is peculiar. Brian's Aunt Methyl is proud to assert that she has never in her fifty-something years traveled farther south than the Kennebec

River. None of the Turners understand why Brian left Maine in the first place, let alone brought back someone from Brooklyn. So it wasn't about my being gay, it was about my *not* being from Maine.

At the end of the honeymoon in Provincetown, we went to visit Brian's mother, Germaine Hortense Turner, and her second husband, Bert. In the middle of a Friday afternoon, we drove our rental car to Lake Cobbossee, where Germaine and Bert maintained a camp: four bedrooms, two fireplaces, assorted living rooms, a dock, and an enclosed porch. It was impeccably neat, with understated antiques, lots of pewter, and a stern nautical motif.

Brian found a note, in precise lavender script, on the kitchen table:

From the Desk of Germaine Hortense Turner, RN

Brian

Bert is at the boat shop. Senator Mitchell has an appointment with me. Make yourself comfortable. There is food in the refrigerator. EAT!

Love,

Mum

Brian smiled and headed for the pantry, where Germaine kept the crackers, and then to the fridge, where she still stored the American cheese slices on the left-hand side of the top shelf, which is the exact same place Brian puts it in our refrigerator. While Brian nibbled, I walked out to the porch and relaxed, watching the sailboats on the lake. The first year together, Brian and I did everything as a unit: ate meals, watched *Star Trek*, panicked about the rent. But as time went by, we felt comfortable enough to diverge: he watches Disney videos while I do needlepoint. He bakes bread while I read cheap science fiction. We have mastered the art of being apart together. So while he nibbled, I relaxed.

The view from the porch took in a blue lake with mahogany boats and a little green island with a little white lighthouse. The only lighthouse I have ever seen on a freshwater lake. I like this lighthouse. I don't know why it's there. I mean, the lake is not big enough to get lost on or anything, but they keep this red lamp burning in the tower all night long. One winter, when Brian and I drove up for a Currier and Ives Christmas, we skated out to the island so that I could see the building close up. Snow covered the brick and the windows were cracked, but the red lamp in the tower burned still. I think that little beacon is kind of a symbol for me. Family is a bit like that: no matter the season, there is always a light out there that tells you where home is.

That summer after Provincetown I sat and watched the lighthouse and the trees around Lake Cobbossee. I listened to the lapping of the lake against the house. After a while I dozed.

I awoke to hear soft but precise steps approaching. The sunlight had shifted and Germaine Hortense stood in front of me. Straight gray hair and sensible steel glasses. Besides chairing the Maine State Board of Nursing, in her spare time, she serves as a full colonel in the United States Air Force National Guard, Strategic Air Command, the only woman in New England with that title. If you were playing *Password* and needed to describe her in one word, you would say "formidable." Behind her back, I call her "Colonel Mother-in-Law."

Still groggy, I stood up to greet her, and we hugged in a clumsy way. Germaine felt awkward around homosexuals, except of course for her son Brian, who didn't really count. Lake Cobbossee was an insular part of Maine that recognized only two homosexuals: Ulysses and Winthrop, known to the town as Huff 'n Puff—purple scarves, topiary bushes, Judy Garland albums, lace tablecloths, Bette Davis videos, lots of jewelry. The kind of old queenery I aspire to. From a statistical perspective, there must be more gays in central Maine than Huff 'n Puff, but none have ever been found, probably because Huff 'n Puff's bakery has been vandalized no fewer than thirteen times. Germaine bakes her own bread, so she never had a lot of interaction with either Huff or Puff.

When Brian first introduced me as his life partner to her, she tightened the corners of her lips and frowned. Brian's brother has been married three times, but each of his wives was not only a woman, but more importantly, born in Maine.

"Where is my kid?" she asked.

"I just woke up. I don't know exactly." My best guess would be sneaking a cigarette somewhere, a habit of his which, despite the fact that I do not smoke, she has always blamed on me.

"Oh." Pause. Pause. The silence thumped against my chest.

Desperate to keep the conversation going, I babbled, "The trip was nice. We saw the Old Man of the Mountain."

"Oh." Pause. Pause. Pause.

Rule number one of small talk: When the conversation lags, ask lots of questions. It gets the air pumping in the other person's lungs. "How was the Senator?"

"Distracted, as Democrats usually are during an election year."

No, not politics. No religion. No politics. Another line of dish. "Hector and Alma visited this summer." Hector is the ex-husband who fathered Brian. "It was nice for us to have family visit."

"You mean Brian's family." Germaine counted family as people from the same gene pool, a pool located somewhere in Maine.

Before I could explain my own theory, Germaine's husband, Bert, walked through the door. "Look who I found out back, sneaking a cigarette!" Bert does not believe in vices. He does not smoke, eats only low-fat food, and runs five miles a day. He drinks no alcohol, except of course for martinis, which are apparently in their own category. Ten years older than Germaine, he is balding and wiry, with the cunning blue eyes and weathered facial lines of a coastal fisherman.

Brian, sheepishly putting out a Marlboro, walked in and said, "Hello, Mum." He hugged her and kissed her on the cheek.

"How is my kid?" Suddenly, she gushed with small talk: convalescent homes, Jean Auel books, and the divorces of both Aunt Methyl and Aunt Dot, punctuating the talk with her decaffeinated coffee whitened with nonfat milk.

Hours later, many hours later, we went to bed. As I put on the only pajamas I ever wore, I came to the conclusion, "You know, she tries, but it's just so awkward. She treats me like I'm one of her social work cases."

Brian, half asleep, replied, "You, of course, are perfect and make it so easy for her."

The night had turned brisk. I hurried under the blanket. "What do you mean by that?"

"What I mean is, you treat her like you are afraid of her."

"I am." There was just an edge of cold wind that made the night splendid. I rubbed my cold feet against his ankles, which he hates. On nights like that, I missed Miss Grrrrl, who doubles as a space heater. I wondered how Miss Grrrrl was doing, spending the weekend with my cousin Kitty. We are the kind of queens who keep Pekingeses, like Russian empresses in an Hercule Poirot mystery. We spoil Miss Grrrrl awfully, with no apologies. Kitty, however, despises the breed, insisting that as self-respecting gay men we ought to own something butch, like a Rottweiler.

"She's really just a nice middle-aged lady from Maine."

"She's a colonel in the air force. How did she treat your other boyfriends?"

"I never had other boyfriends."

Major difference. I am the only man Brian has ever dated, whereas, by my own rough count, over fifty men have enjoyed the pleasure of my company. My list includes a lumberjack, a priest, a Ringling Brothers circus clown, a Mafia hit man, and a cowboy named Theodore. Kitty used to call me the demolition derby of gay romance.

"You mean she has never met anyone you even dated?"

"Well, there was Nadine West. Senior year of Hebron Academy. Now, she was true trailer park trash. That kind of backwoods Maine family where everyone is their own first cousin. Enormous buck teeth and high hair. We dated for about six weeks, in my brief flirtation with heterosexuality. She was so afraid of Mum that she wouldn't even dial my number. Mum used to say, 'Nadine *seems* very nice, but she doesn't have any backbone. Are you sure she was born in Maine?'"

Sleep crept over the small talk. I dreamt of buck-toothed women and the lighthouse. Never blinking.

On Saturday morning, Brian and I awoke to the sound of pans clattering and the smell of tepid decaf. Germaine made enough noise downstairs to let us know that she did not approve of sleeping much past dawn, even on a weekend. She served toast on the porch. Brian has an irrational fear of breakfast, one of those dancer things, so he chewed on the crust a little, before slipping the slices onto my plate when his mother wasn't looking. I have that doughnut-eating cop mentality: if it's on your plate, eat it. Some people say the secret of our happy marriage is that I eat for him.

Before the second sip of coffee, Germaine got to the point. "Bert has invited some of his friends for supper tonight. The Ridlows. Sort of a come-as-you-are party. Very informal." Her brows fretted unmercifully. She went into the kitchen to start cooking.

I asked Brian, "So, if it's a come-as-you-are party, why does she look nervous?"

Brian replied, "Bert invited friends that he made while married to his first wife, Patti, the debutante. Mr. and Mrs. Ridlow are nasty rich. Their family rode luxury class on the *Mayflower*."

At 7:30 A.M. sharp, the vacuum whined as Germaine cleaned up before the maid could get there. Brian sneaked off for a cigarette. As I stumbled toward the bathroom, Germaine handed me a slip of paper. It started with "From the Desk of Germaine Hortense Turner, RN" and continued on in her precise lavender script. "I've made you a list of errands. After you get out of the bathroom, of course."

Brian and I hurried off to our errands. At the Augusta Market we picked up wines I couldn't pronounce, as well as butter and bread and sour cream and a dozen assorted items. We picked up a floral arrangement at La Verdiere's. But we saved our favorite task for last. We stopped off at the Lakeshore Antique Shop. Germaine had told us to pick up mismatched platters, bone china, so that the whole event would have the feeling of "come-as-you-are."

China is a big thing to Brian and me. When we first met, I worked in the Tabletop Department at Macy's in downtown Newark, New Jersey. We used to meet for lunch a lot in those first days, when we couldn't get enough time with each other. One day, he waited for me as I struggled with a particularly persnickety bride who refused to find a pattern suitable for her mauve dining room. Her groom sighed after the first thousand discards, and I knew that divorce lawyers lay in wait. But Brian waited around patiently, and forty-five minutes later, as we walked off for a fifteen-minute lunch he said, "By the way, the final *Jeopardy* answer is Virtue."

"Virtue?"

"And the question, of course, is, 'What will Brian and Kevin's china pattern be when they grow up and get married?'"

And it was, of course. Poor as we were, the day we moved into the studio apartment on Brunswick Street I purchased a platter with the white rose against a pale blue background and a silver border. And the platter became the signal for an occasion. Any time we have ever celebrated a big event—Brian getting a role in a show, me getting a promotion, Miss Grrrl's first birthday (*the Feast of the Beast*), we served up dinner on that bone china platter. You'd be surprised how much better macaroni and cheese tastes when served on bone china. As the years passed, we did not get much less poor, but we did add plates and bowls and salt shakers. So, even though we don't own a home or a car, or even a second pair of sneakers, we can now serve high dinner for eight on the rickety slab of dining room table that I won in a particularly ugly divorce with a nameless ex-lover. In the hands of better caretakers, it could have been an antique. We, however, lost the screws that attached the base to the table, and Miss Grrrl picked one of those legs as her favorite chew toy. Some people say that the secret of our long-term commitment is that we've ignored a tidy household in favor of keeping a happy dog instead.

Rather than looking elegant, our dining room table just crowds our studio apartment. But the top of the table sits resplendent with gleaming blue and white china. It takes a long-term relationship to collect sixty-odd pieces of matching china. So whenever we shop for china, it's like falling in love all over again.

At the commitment ceremony, we wouldn't let anyone give us china or gifts. We had built our own home, and we would fill it our own way. Our crystal consisted of a hodgepodge of Welch's grape jelly jars. And our flatware consisted of two sets of matching chopsticks.

At Lakeshore Antiques, we examined every piece of porcelain in the place and eventually settled upon four dishes with patterns that would complement Germaine's dining room.

We returned to the camp for more chores. Since Germaine was throwing a "casual" dinner party, we set the picnic table in china on a lace tablecloth. I even learned how to fold a napkin. Germaine sent us to shower in shifts.

After my shower, I walked downstairs in the Ralph Lauren shirt I had purchased to impress her. Germaine dressed as casually as she ever got: a cream linen skirt with a lavender silk blouse. Bert wore jeans, a red polo shirt, and an apron that said, "Rule #1: Only the Captain's Wife Can Make the Captain Cook."

Around six, that year's black Saab roared down the driveway and parked behind our rented red compact. As a mature couple walked in, Germaine said, "Thanks for coming. You all remember my son Brian." Pause. Pause. Pause. She looked at me with the closest she ever got to panic. Emily Post had never discussed the etiquette of introducing the non-Yankee gay lover of one's oldest son from a previous marriage to the friends of one's second husband's first wife at an informal dinner party.

I rushed in with "And I'm Kevin," with no explanation. Like I had appeared from the foam on the lake. I extended my hand to shake but found only empty air.

Mr. Ridlow stared at my hand with grim concern. He said, "I'm Mr. Ridlow and this is Mrs. Ridlow." They both nodded their heads. Mr. and Mrs. Ridlow wore coordinated sailing outfits, broad navy blue and white stripes to accent their Florida tans and their painstakingly thin figures.

Bert said to Mr. Ridlow, "While I go drown those lobsters, why don't you fix us drinks?" Brian walked off with Bert, while Mr. Ridlow fixed perfect martinis.

This left us little women to bask in the appetizers on the porch. Mrs. Ridlow murmured, "Gerry . . ."

"Germaine."

"Yes, quite. Germaine, you have so many quaint ways of flavoring sour cream. You should have tasted those puff pastries that Patti used to make!"

Germaine thrust a carrot into the clam dip. "Of course, Patti didn't work for a living." A small black fiberglass boat shot past the lighthouse. Noisily.

"Yes, Patti knew enough to stay home and take care of her husband."

"Which, of course, explains her divorce."

"And you working as a nurse," Mrs. Ridlow continued. "Bert has several doctors in his family, but you're the first nurse. If I did not know better, I would say you married him for his money."

I couldn't resist. "Whereas it's obvious that Mr. Ridlow married you for your charm." Mrs. Ridlow paused, but it was evident that she was pointedly ignoring the fact that I sat in the room, as if I had passed gas.

"And you raised those two boys on your own. Now, Brian is some kind of chorus boy, right?"

"Dance captain. In a Broadway show," I pointed out.

"How charming. But is there a future in that?" Mrs. Ridlow asked earnestly.

As the fiberglass boat roared past us again, the first round of drinks were delivered. Mr. Ridlow announced, "That boat is chopping too hard. The engine isn't riveted right."

We sipped the martinis in awkward silence. Sure enough, on the boat's third cross of the lake, the motor fell right into the water. "Besides that," Mr. Ridlow announced, "the driver was from New Hampshire." This led the Ridlows to discuss the other foreigners on the lake.

Another round of martinis. We sat staring at the lighthouse, waiting for it to blink, waiting for dinner. Soon Bert served steaming lobsters with melted butter and sweet corn. I felt an etiquette attack coming on. No one had ever served lobsters in my neighborhood in Brooklyn. Brian saw my confusion and lifted a utensil (which he later identified as a shellfish pick) in a pointed manner. "What lovely lobsters," Germaine announced. I watched Brian to figure out which parts were edible.

"Where did you get them, Bert?" Brian asked.

"Miller's," Bert said, scowling at the fact that I had just squirted lobster juice all over my Ralph Lauren shirt.

Mrs. Ridlow unfolded a napkin over her immaculate lap. "Normally, Mr. Ridlow and I only eat seafood that we ourselves have caught. It seems like such a waste to have that perfectly good boat and not use it for anything."

I had just yanked some white fleshy stuff from a claw and dunked it into the butter when Mrs. Ridlow asked, "Do you trawl?"

"Trawl?" I wondered whether trawl meant that I had spilled butter on my shoe. Brian responded to my quizzical look by saying, "We don't own a boat. There isn't any great yachting in Jersey City."

"Oh, that's too bad," Mrs. Ridlow commiserated. "Is that where you're from? I thought that you spoke with a distinct accent."

I replied, "Well, actually, I was raised in Brooklyn, but awl us tuff guys tawk like dis." Brian's boot savaged my shin under the table.

"Oh, that's in New York, " Mrs. Ridlow sighed. "An awful city. Much worse than Boston. Mr. Ridlow and I went to New York last fall. On business. There aren't any nice hotels there."

"It was Halloween," Mr. Ridlow said, "and the town was full of drunks. It was worse than those Micks on Saint Patrick's Day."

Germaine said, pointedly, "Would you pass the salt, please?"

"And the costumes, people exposing themselves in ways no God-fearing Christian would show them—"

"Would someone pass the corn, please?" Germaine interrupted, shoulders braced visibly.

Mr. Ridlow continued, "But the most disgusting thing was all those boys dressed up in wigs and dresses. If I were you, Gerry—"

"Germaine," I corrected.

"I would worry about Brian living even near that town. It just might turn him queer."

Crack. Colonel Germaine Hortense Turner's shellfish pick slapped against the bone china plate. Everyone stopped, lobster halfway to their mouths. Brian sucked in his breath. Even the lighthouse blinked. She spoke in a voice so low that we all had to lean in to hear her above the sound of the lapping lake: "Well, Kent Ridlow, perhaps you would now care to hear my opinion of backwoods Maine lumberjacks who have more money than brains."

The evening passed with morbid quiet.

Later that night, after the Ridlows had departed and the dishes were done, I went out on the porch to relax. The loons sang their crazy song, the crickets chirped their crazy chirps. And the lighthouse lamp glowed red.

Brian came out with two glasses of wine.

"Nice night," I said, and then we lapsed into the contented silence of two people who had known each other for years and didn't have to fill the spaces with small talk. Moonlight danced on the water.

Germaine Hortense walked out a few minutes later. "Kevin, I want to apologize for the Ridlows. I thought we were all more civilized than that."

"No need, " I said, "but thanks for saying something, Germaine." We both fumbled with wine glasses, still not knowing how to hug.

As the three of us looked at the lighthouse, Germaine smiled to Brian, "I'm so glad that you didn't marry Nadine West."

Seven years into the relationship, Brian got an offer to dance with ODC/San Francisco. I was tired of selling china at Macy's anyway, so we loaded up a Ryder truck with five thousand pounds of books, milk crates, china, and Pekingeses. Four weeks before we moved, Miss Grrrrl gave birth to six puppies, including Wolfcub and Diva. So, in the hot August sun, two adult queens, one adult Pekingese, and six nursing puppies climbed into the cab of the truck and began the great western migration. We traveled through the South and then the West, leaving a puppy behind wherever we stayed the night. Kind of like Johnny Appleseed, only with Pekingeses.

This is our thirteenth year together. I am now the longest surviving in-law in the Turner family, although we don't get back east as much since moving to the coast gauche. I became a deputy sheriff, mostly because Brian believed I could. He rehearses during the day, I patrol the county by night. Some say the secret of our happy marriage is in the scheduling.

Sometimes we fight about the trivia of our lives, who should walk Miss Grrrrl, who had the right answer on *Jeopardy*, whether to put blue or white lights on the Christmas tree. Kitty once told me never to divorce Brian, because although I would get all the charm in the settlement, he surely would get all the looks. Anyway, the fights help keep us together because they show us we both care about home. Sometimes a long-term relationship is just about making a long-term relationship work.

Sometimes a long-term relationship is about perspective. It is about my knowing that he thought he gave a bad performance even though both *The Chronicle* and *The Examiner* critics raved about him. It is about my rushing home to tell him about an arrest or him playing Fritz in *The Nutcracker* with Berkeley Ballet, or about *The Sentinel* finally publishing an article I wrote. Sometimes a long-term relationship is about the triumphs shared.

And in the end we know that come Thanksgiving, we will put an orange tablecloth on top of that rickety old table, just because Kitty will fly out for the holiday and Kitty hates orange. ("Honestly, you two queens. Can't you even decorate the table without being flamboyant?") We will put eight bone china plates on that table, eight Virtues that we have collected over the years, as well as a bowl full of Virtue on the floor for Miss Grrrrl, Wolfcub, and Diva. Miss Grrrrl knows that we never put Alpo into a bowl of Virtue. No, on holidays she gets the good stuff.

On the table, there will be four Flintstones glasses, three Superman glasses, and even a Scooby Doo glass. We're even gonna put out those matching chopsticks.

The day after Thanksgiving, we will wake Kitty up out of a sound sleep and demand that she take our Christmas card picture. With all of those Pekingeses.

A few weeks ago, a package arrived in the mail from Maine to the both of us. The lavender-inked note in it read:

A wedding present, a few years late. I guess that patience is also a Virtue. I was too late for the china, so let me start you on the silver. Shellfish picks, to go with the lobster. If the yachting in San Francisco is any better than in Jersey City.
Love to you both, Mum.

Brian smiled, held up the sterling, and said, "I wonder how Kitty is gonna eat lasagna with this."

We will never be as rich as the Ridlows. Instead, we may become the next Huff 'n Puff. There is no doubt that we will always live together. We will eventually own a full service for eight. Someday, Brian and I will retire together, maybe to the lake, where the lighthouse never blinks.

Terry Colbert
and James Mason

- t w o -

supportive relations

T E R R Y G. C O L B E R T

Christmas Eve, 1977. Father and I were seated across from each other at the kitchen table, sipping rounds of the gin-and-tonics he called my Hemingway specials because I made them with a splash of Angostura bitters and a lemon twist, the way Thomas Hudson liked them in *Islands in the Stream.* We had a tradition that in my role as house bartender I always mixed the first round. After that, it was "every man for himself."

Father had been smoking cigarettes since Hoover was in office, and in 1977 I was still smoking too. So there was an ashtray in the middle of the table, flanked by his Pall Malls and my Benson and Hedges. Mother was cutting and chopping at the counter between the sink and the range, prepping side dishes for the traditional meal the three of us would share after opening our gifts the next day. She didn't smoke, and her diabetes made it risky for her to drink alcohol. She may have been sipping a sugar-free soft drink, or her hands may have been too busy for that, I don't recall. But I do know she was an active participant in our conversation. We were a verbal family, and talk was the main event whenever we got together. Oscar Wilde, whose tales Father read to me before I was old enough to read for myself, remarks in *The Selfish Giant* that after visiting his friend the Cornish ogre for seven

17

years, the giant had said all he had to say, "for his conversation was limited." My parents and I never had that problem.

Through the late 1960s and early '70s, while I was in college and graduate school, we had talked inexhaustibly. On long drives, at home, in restaurants, in campus bars. About politics and religion, about literature and music, about the war and the peace movement. About sex, drugs, and rock and roll. You name it. We had been "completely open and honest," as the phrase went in the era of Nehru jackets and T-groups, freely discussing whatever came to mind, following ideas wherever they led.

Only where my own love life was concerned had I been less than candid. The "sex" in our discussions had always been other people's sex—norms in flux and all that—never my own. I was thirty-one and unmarried, but I had dated plenty of women and my parents assumed that I was straight. I was careful not to disturb that assumption.

I had been out to myself, in the sense of falling consciously in love with guy after guy, since junior high school. Old Oscar had helped me avoid the self-loathing that gays are prey to, or rather I had been assisted in self-affirmation by the knowledge that Father admired the work of a man who went to jail for being queer. But in terms of overt sexual activity, my coming out had been a slow and tentative process. And in terms of public visibility, or being out to anyone but my secret sharers, it had scarcely begun. Prior to September 21, 1977, I had assumed—like many gay men of my generation—that I would take my secret to my grave. I would excel artistically or professionally and make everyone in my family proud of me, I might marry a companionable woman and sire children upon her while fantasizing about men, but I would never allow myself to be branded publicly as a homosexual. Pilloried in the public square with a capital H on my chest? No, thank you.

In the last year or two, the duplicity and mendacity of closeted living had begun to take their toll, and I had been increasingly prone to depression. In my studio apartment at the University of Illinois, I had lain awake many a night remembering the men I had loved but had dared not touch for fear of blowing my cover. In the daytime I was a doctoral candidate in English and a teacher of rhetoric and poetry. At night I was a habitué of bars and after-hours parties, looking but rarely leaping, almost always going home alone. Occasionally another man's knee would brush mine under a table, and we would slink off to a furtive tumble between his sheets or mine—followed by the fear of discovery, the resolve never to give in again, and the avoidance of the man who was now an accessory.

Sometime during the Bicentennial Year, as I sat in Murphy's Pub listening to Billy Joel sing "The Piano Man" for the thousandth time, the conviction gripped me like the cold hand of death that the life I'd led myself some sixteen years was coming to an end. Unable to move out into the "real world" as a conventional husband and father, I had taken refuge on the game preserve called graduate school for about as long as was credible. All that lay ahead, unless I made a major change, was a moribund career in equivocation, evasion, deception, and lies.

In September 1977, in an attempt to save myself from the death that begins with the spirit before it tells on the body, I left the graduate program at the University of Illinois and entered Garrett-Evangelical Theological Seminary on the campus of Northwestern University in Evanston. I told myself and others that I was getting back in touch with my roots, that I was melding my mother's religious influence with my father's literary influence, and that I would emerge as a literate divine in the style of Northrup Frye. These were genuine aims, but they also served as rationalizations for an existential decision that I could not discuss openly. Evanston was the last exit before the River Styx.

On Monday of orientation week, during a break in one of the meetings, I met several new students around an ashtray in the hall. Among them was James Mason, whose name stuck with me by association with the actor who played Captain Nemo in Disney's *Twenty Thousand Leagues under the Sea*. This Mason had a beard too, plus a dark brown mane and wire-rims that appealed to my Beatles-bred sensibilities, but I was no more turned on to him than to half a dozen other guys in the meeting. *Star Wars* had come out earlier that year, and the guy who really caught my eye was a Mark Hamill look-alike in a far corner of the room. It was to stalk him that I attended a dorm party the following Thursday evening, September 21.

Early in the evening, Jim Mason and I made a booze run in his VW hatchback, down Sheridan Road to Howard Street, which was the line of demarcation between dry Evanston and wet Chicago. I assumed that he was straight, and I did my best to act like an all-right guy. I talked about Hemingway a lot. We came back to the dorm, laden with potables, and I went on shadowing my Luke Skywalker. After a while, I began to worry that I might spook him. Better give him some space, I thought. Looking around the room, I spotted Jim sitting alone on the sofa. I joined him and shared the ashtray on the coffee table. Our hands rested on our knees while we smoked and tippled, leaning forward to flick an ash or pick a can up, and by chance the knuckles of our little fingers brushed. Most guys would have drawn back. Neither of us did. After a second's hesitation, I felt a light rubbing. My pulse quickened with the rush of recognition that only queers can know—the sole perk of closeted living. When I rubbed back, ever so lightly, the accidental brush became a signal.

We glanced at each other once, reassuringly, and then Jim stood up and walked out to the john between the suites. I counted to ten, lest it appear we were leaving together, and followed him. At the sinks, we spoke to each other briefly in the mirror.

"How's it goin'?"

"Fine."

Turning into each other, we embraced. I nuzzled his neck. We kissed.

"Is this you or the beer?" he asked suspiciously.

"It's me," I assured him "It's me."

We stepped back into the party to allay suspicion and then headed for his room in the dorm next door. Twenty minutes later, while he was reclining on the sofa bed and I was going down on him, I felt a seismic rumble in his stomach and pulled back instinctively, just in time to watch the turkey tetrazzini from dinner come cascading down his hairy chest along with the beer he hadn't digested.

"Sorry about that," he said.

I grabbed a damp cloth from his bathroom and helped him clean up.

"We'll try again tomorrow night, okay?" I suggested.

It was okay with him, and it was so okay with both of us from then on that I spent every night in his room. My bed, in the suite I shared with another seminarian, served to fold laundry and stack papers. My roommate thought for several months that I had a woman off campus somewhere.

Each morning through October, November, and early December, I crawled out of Jim's bed, got dressed, and went back to my dorm to shower before breakfast and classes or walked downtown to my part-time job at Chandler's Bookstore. I thought about him—about us, increasingly—while I rang up purchases, often with the strains of Princess Leia's theme running through my head. At night, when I wasn't in the library or in his room, I sat on the rocks overlooking Lake Michigan and thought about my life. Knowing now which way my bliss led, I ached deeper than ever before with the sickness Hemingway said you got when you lied about the things that mattered most to you. As I watched the lights of ships cruising into Chicago and studied the reflection of the stars in the black water, listening to the deep surge of the lake, I considered that the downward way and the upward way might indeed be one. I was ready to die to the old life of duplicity and be born into another, utterly unpredictable, which I envisioned as franker and therefore easier. All that held me back was the discomfiture I had so long avoided inflicting on my parents. In the final analysis, reflecting upon the belief that those who are with God must know what God knows, I reasoned that I could either reveal myself to my parents while they were alive or stand revealed in a far harsher light later. It would be better in the end, I thought, to have lived honestly with them in the meantime.

One evening shortly before the winter holidays, over a pitcher of German beer in the Valhalla Lounge in Skokie, I told Jim: "I don't know how many years I have left. All the smoking, the drinking, the late nights. . . . God knows, I haven't courted longevity. None of us knows when the final moment will come, of course. But when it comes for me, I would like you to be there to hold my hand." He swayed slightly, as though recoiling from a surprise punch, but in a moment he recovered and said yes, he was willing to give it a try. Be partners. As long as it seemed a healthy relationship for both of us. As long as neither of us felt it was turning destructive or becoming detrimental to our ultimate good. Jim still identified as an evangelical Christian back then and told me that if he ever had to choose between me and Jesus, I would lose. Neither of us knew whether the partnership was going to work.

The conversation at home that Christmas Eve ran from my studies at Garrett to my plans for the New Year's Day service I was slated to conduct for the hometown congregation, with Jim Mason serving as reader. My parents had met him on a visit to Evanston in October. Later they told me they thought it odd that he accompanied us while we toured the Baha'i Temple in Wilmette and had dinner downtown, but I had formed strong friendships with classmates before and they never guessed that Jim and I had been sleeping together. When our pastor asked me to lead the New Year's Day service and I asked Jim to assist me, my parents invited him to stay at our house the night before the service. In a day or two, I would be driving down to Wood River and bringing him back up to Galesburg. My latest lover was going to see the new year in with my parents and me and was going to sleep with me under my parents' roof. To my mind, what had long been a sin of omission—not telling as long as they didn't ask—was about to become a sin of commission, an outright deception. I could not allow that.

From the church I had grown up in, the conversation moved to memories of Christmases past and the abundance we had enjoyed as a family. I recalled the flood a couple of years earlier that had damaged a number of possessions in my apartment at the University of Illinois, including some of the cherished LPs that my parents had given me for Christmas over the years. The flood had reinforced an important truth, I said: The material gifts, which were perishable, had never been more than symbols of the spiritual and indestructible gift of love.

"Over the years," I said, drawing a deep breath and speaking as evenly as I could, "we've given each other many wonderful gifts. This year I want to give you the gift of truth."

Then I told them that Jim Mason and I were much more than friends, that we had been lovers since September, and that we intended to stay together as partners for life. Father's face went blank a moment while Mother laid a spoon down on the range and came to the table, wiping her hands on her apron. Hardly a minute had elapsed, however, before he extended his hand across the table. "You're the same person you were five minutes ago," he said as we shook hands, "the same son we've taken pride in for thirty-one years. We just know you better now and will be able to understand your motives and actions better."

All my life, my parents had told me their love for me was unconditional. I had believed that they meant what they said, but I had doubted that they had taken all the possibilities into account. There was one revelation, I had feared, that their love could not withstand. On that Christmas Eve and in the months and years that followed, they showed how needless my fear had been. They were concerned about the hurdles Jim and I would have to clear, about the hostility we might encounter, and about the professional and economic cost of coming out. But there was never a hint of aversion for my sexuality or of abatement in their regard for me. Their love never wavered. They welcomed Jim into our home, embraced him as kin ("I feel like I've gained a son," my mother remarked once), and together with his mother and grandmother created an expanded family around our partnership.

Jim had been the child of an unwed teenager. "It's the old story about 'The Quarterback and the Cheerleader,'" he liked to say. The Masons had adopted him in infancy, perhaps in the hope that having a child to raise would help their marriage, but it hadn't helped enough. Their marital road had been rocky from the start and had led to divorce when he was about eleven. The adoptive mother, Dorothy, had been given custody.

When I drove down to Wood River a few days after Christmas to fetch Jim for the New Year's Day service, Dorothy met me at their front door, looking down at me through the screen, and admitted me to the house with barely an acknowledgment of my greeting. He had been working at his own coming-out for several years and had confided to her long before we met that he had "homosexual tendencies," but he had discussed them as a conservative Christian in terms of coping and celibacy. Now he was talking about a spousal relationship with another man, and with that she was quite unhappy. For her, however, the problem was not principally a religious one. She was a more mainstream Protestant in those days than Jim, who had undergone conversion as a phase of self-definition in college, and she probably cared less than he did about the compatibility of Christian doctrine and the "gay lifestyle." Her difficulty in accepting our partnership stemmed from a secular understanding of what real men and real women were supposed to be, colored by a penchant for Tarzan stories and for Elvis Presley's music.

Dorothy viewed me initially, I suppose, as the older queer who was leading her sexually confused son down the road to ruin. But even as it dawned on her that I was a fundamentally sound person and that Jim and I were equal partners in forging our peculiar way of life, she remained unable to see the love of two men as reason to rejoice. My parents started sending us anniversary cards the first year, but Dorothy dismissed the occasion with the remark that there was "nothing to celebrate." Her loyalty to Jim was simple, tacit, and automatic, as was her generosity, and in the long run we both benefited from her largesse in many ways. But she never accepted our partnership as a moral alternative to marriage, and she never warmed up to me personally. I believe that she was alternately intimidated and annoyed by the intellectualism I had acquired as a perennial graduate student. I know that she was ill at ease in discussion of the animated kind I was accustomed to at home. Confrontation frightened her. In the face of conflict, her typical reaction was a surly "I don't want to talk about it!" followed by withdrawal. Her faith in conflict resolution lay buried in the rubble of her marriage. At times, she seemed to read some kind of class conflict into our differences. My roots are solidly proletarian, but my mother was a master at introducing touches of elegance into the home on a tight budget and I am much like her. The last time I tried to set the table for Dorothy, though, before we sat down to something from the microwave, she actually yelled at me, "Don't fold the napkins!"

What transformed the strained relationship between Dorothy, Jim, and me into a viable family relationship was my parents' intervention. Within the first year, they took the opportunity of a long weekend in St. Louis to call Dorothy and pay her a visit. The common ground they proposed was that their son and hers were gay and were lovers—or were partners, as the two would have it. As the parents of the pair, they might as well get to know each other. "We all want to do whatever's best for our children," I can imagine my mother saying, over the phone in their motel room. "It's really in their interests for us to keep the lines of communication open."

The meeting went well. Dorothy and my father found they shared a wry sense of humor. They were only about three years apart in age, he had been a Depression-era vagrant straight out of Steinbeck, and she was a former Marine who had joined the service chiefly to get away from an unhappy home. As alums of the College of Hard Knocks, they had a lot in common. My mother had one of those sunny dispositions that nothing can becloud, and she was a compulsive correspondent. When she and Dorothy discovered they both were diabetic, a card-and-note friendship sprang up that lasted as long as both of them lived.

Also involved in our unconventional family was Jim's grandmother by marriage, Mary Catherine, who had once been Dorothy's father's secretary. Years after the death of Dorothy's mother, the former secretary and former-boss-now-widower had crossed paths at a supermarket checkout and had discovered a previously unexplored compatibility. Mary Catherine was a devout Catholic and might have been expected to object strongly to my partnership with Jim. Whether she was moved principally by love for Dorothy and Jim, by respect for my parents, or by her understanding of Christian charity, I do not know, but she was unfailingly gracious from the first time I met her. She always greeted me with an embrace, a veritable *pax*, and presided over our meals together with the quiet determination that they should go smoothly. Like Dorothy, she became a regular correspondent with my mother.

Jim's adoptive father, Wayne, had remarried and was living near Atlanta. Shortly after the holidays, Jim came out to him over the phone. I doubt that Wayne had time to assimilate the news, and I know he never had the opportunity to meet me or to grasp the depth of our commitment. Early in 1978 he suffered a fatal heart attack. I drove Jim to O'Hare for his flight to southern Illinois, where the funeral and burial took place, but I chose not to attend. A black comedy of sorts unfolded as the airline misrouted the body to Chicago and had to ship it back, while relatives from two marriages grieved near St. Louis. I heard all about it from Jim. With Wayne Mason's second family, however, I attempted no contact.

The willingness of my parents, Dorothy, and Mary Catherine to be friends created a background of supportive relations for Jim and me while we were occupied in the foreground with coming out and learning to live together. In the spring of 1978, we came out formally to the United Methodist Church and Garrett-Evangelical Theological Seminary, with the consequence that Jim's diaconal orders were revoked and my candidacy for ordination was canceled. A number of friends had counseled us to stay in the closet for the sake of our ministries, and our bishop subsequently told us that had we conferred with him privately, we might have been accommodated despite the prohibitive language of the Discipline. But we were embarked on a new life of honesty, and we reasoned that were we ordained on the condition of secrecy and given charges miles apart, we would be ensnared in a life of hypocrisy and furtive assignations leading inevitably to exposure. The scandal of being found out after we became the moral leaders of Christian congregations would be far messier than anything we faced as gay seminarians.

The seminary administration and faculty wrestled for several weeks over whether to let us continue work on our master of divinity degrees when we were no longer eligible for ordination. One of the considerations was economic. The Discipline of the United Methodist Church forbade the disbursement of funds to any agency that condoned homosexual relationships, and Garrett was receiving upwards of seven figures a year from the church. In plenary session one day in May, the faculty decided by a narrow vote (14 for us, 15 against) to deny us further academic credit. The news went out through the campus paper at Northwestern to the Chicago-area media and the wire services, we made page two of the *New York Times*, and a camera crew from CBS showed up to interview us and follow us through the cafeteria line, perhaps on the hunch that our food choices would reveal something about us. For a year or so, we became a cause célèbre between Garrett and Northwestern, testing their cooperative graduate program, due to the support we received from a number of Northwestern faculty and students. While the air was still heavy with the smoke of fire and counterfire, however, the two of us had retired from the field. We left Evanston and moved downstate to Champaign-Urbana, my stomping grounds as an undergraduate and graduate at the University of Illinois, to find real jobs and get acquainted. We had known each other only a few months, after all, and still could not say whether our partnership would last the first year, no matter how shoulder-to-shoulder we tried to look for the cameras.

We were coming out at a time of rapidly increasing gay and lesbian visibility everywhere, and we did our part for public education in Champaign-Urbana by making ourselves available to the local media for talk shows and by being out to all of our friends, employers, and coworkers. Our commitment to gay rights and our determination to present a united front as a gay couple helped us weather the conflicts as we explored each other's personalities. It would have been far easier for us to go our separate ways, however, had it not been for the family ties that grew up around our partnership. My parents were frequent visitors at our successive apartments, Jim and I spent holidays and getaway weekends in Galesburg or southern Illinois, and we all shared a Thanksgiving at Mary Catherine's home in Alton. The foot problems that came with diabetes affected Dorothy and my mother differently and made it more difficult for Dorothy to travel, but she and Mary Catherine did manage a visit to my parents' home in Galesburg once, as part of an itinerary that allowed Jim and me to chauffeur Dorothy on a tour of her alma mater, Bradley University, in nearby Peoria. The support of our four closest relatives created a presumption of acceptance in the rest of the family, especially on my side, where there had always been more networking than on Jim's, and there was never any question of our welcome as a couple at family gatherings. The expectation that we would stay together seemed to develop early on, and it gave us something to save when the two of us were at odds.

The family event in which I took the greatest pride was the day in 1988 when the six of us—Mother, Father, Dorothy, Mary Catherine, Jim, and I—gathered for commencement at the University of Illinois as Jim received his master's in library science. He had earned the degree patiently, taking a unit or half-unit a semester while working full-time at the

Urbana Free Library. On my way to fetch the car after the ceremony, walking down the street on one of those halcyon spring days that grace the Midwest after the ordeal of winter, I thought what an improbable convergence it was, our coming together from diverse backgrounds to celebrate Jim's achievement, and what a superachievement we were ourselves.

The job search that followed upon Jim's degree led us from Illinois to Kansas, and the job I lucked into in Kansas has led us to San Francisco. What our life by the Bay may hold, no one can tell. In the words of Sydney Freedman, one of our favorite *M*A*S*H* characters, "We'll see, and then we'll know." But that we are together for as long as we both shall live is as certain as anything can be in this world. We have shared too many of our lives' critical moments, the highs and the lows, the frustrations and the epiphanies, for either of us ever to feel whole again without the other. We are like the sides of a Möbius strip: There's no telling where one leaves off and the other begins.

No ceremony religious or secular has ever been needed to unite us. We have grown together out of the solid ground of daily living. From the outset, each of us deeply wanted a lifetime companionship—Jim perhaps to find something that eluded Dorothy and Wayne Mason, I perhaps to recapitulate something I saw in my parents—and we both embraced ideals of patience and forgiveness that have made it possible. My model for an enduring partnership has been my parents' marriage, and I know from them that whatever sanctions the church or the state may confer, two people who stay together for life do so one day at a time. An institution may bless their commitment at the outset, but it lasts only if they renew it after every crisis, learning from their conflicts instead of being destroyed by them, and reaffirm the love they both believe in.

One of the reasons so many marriages fail, my parents told me, is that young couples misunderstand the nature of love. They think that it is a state of rapture, going on and on, day after day. When they are not enraptured, they are not in love and have to look elsewhere for the real thing. The truth is that rapture comes and goes. It may teach us something of love's conciliatory bent, but love itself is something else. It is an ideal, it guides us like the proverbial star, and fidelity to an ideal is more often a deliberate act than an impulse. In life as a whole, there are flights of ecstasy and fits of anger, moments of greatness and hours of pettiness, successes and failures, joys and sorrows. Sometimes we embrace in exultation at the beauty of a Pacific sunset, sometimes in grief beside a casket. Those who want to live through all these things together may stay together for life. Those who are in it only for the rapture will probably part.

During the years that Jim and I spent in Kansas, our parents began to take their leave of us. Dorothy went first, in 1991, due to the renal failure that diabetics are prone to. My mother started dialysis on Christmas Day of 1993. My father developed emphysema, and in November 1995 he was hospitalized with pneumonia. He recovered enough to be released and to share a room with Mother in the nursing home where they had celebrated their golden wedding anniversary, but on Thanksgiving morning he suffered a heart attack and died. Jim and I spent Christmas selling Mother's piano and boxing up the last of their household goods for the auctioneer.

In January 1996, the loss of circulation to which diabetics are also prone led to infection in Mother's feet, and I authorized her first amputation—the left leg, up to the knee. February brought my job offer at the University of California, San Francisco, and March brought me to the Bay. Jim sold our house in Kansas and rejoined me in June. Mother and I kept in communication by phone through the summer, but by late August she again became "unresponsive" as the infection spread up her right leg. I consented to the second amputation, and from that surgery she never recovered. She suffered a series of strokes, and after a few days her doctor recommended taking her off of dialysis. I flew back to Illinois with Jim to consider her condition first-hand and consult with relatives, and in the end I concurred with the doctor. Jim sat with me by her bed the last few days. On September 8, 1996, she passed away.

We still keep in touch with Mary Catherine. She sends us gift boxes at Christmas, and we remember her with cards and flowers and phone calls on special occasions. Her last words to me as we parted after Dorothy's funeral were "Don't forget me." We haven't, nor have we forgotten the loving support that she and Dorothy and my mother and father gave us all those years while the two of us made a life for ourselves. We will remember it gratefully as we celebrate each anniversary in the city of our dreams.

Chandler Clifton
and John McFarland

-three-

a house of many colors

J O H N M C F A R L A N D

I walk down the street. I catch the eye of somebody interesting. I strike up a conversation. I clear a place for chance to operate. And I see where it takes me. His
name is Chandler. Nice.

Somebody will ask me later, "Well, is it love?"

I definitely know it's fun. I can't be sure of much more at that early stage. I remember
what W. H. Auden wrote in quite another context: "Pleasure is by no means an infallible
critical guide, but it is the least fallible." That settles it: I continue to play it by ear.

Times passes, as it does, and Chandler and I are attending a fund-raiser. A perfectly nice
woman asks me, "How long have you two been together?"

I look up at the ceiling to do the calculations. Then I lower my gaze and lock eyes with
the woman. "Twenty-three . . . ," I start. She's smiling. By the time I finish off my declara-
tion with ". . . years," the smile has evaporated and her jaw has dropped.

"Years?" she asks as if she's misheard me. *"Years?"*

Her astonishment brings me up short. Did she imagine I was taking so long to come up
with an answer in days, weeks, or months?

The woman slowly regains her composure. Retreating into the safety zone of books, she says, "Tolstoy wrote, 'All happy families are alike but an unhappy family is unhappy after its own fashion.' "

I nod as if that has any application whatsoever to my life. I do know that Tolstoy would have to toss that line in the wastebasket if he were writing about people remotely like us. In my mind I try out a possibility for a Tolstoy of today:

In society, people say, "There's been a terrible accident, though fortunately nobody was hurt," but men like Andrei and Petrov have been heard to say, "I was just part of a fabulous accident, and I'm a total wreck!"

That evening at the fund-raiser, I used all my self-control not to share this opening to *Andrei Karenin and His Particular Friend* with the inquiring woman. Instead, I asked if she had ever given chance an opportunity to operate at a critical point in her life.

She looked at me strangely and said, "No!"

"We bought our first house on a lark," I told her. "It turned out to be the best thing we'd ever done together that wasn't sex."

That fixed her. She moved on quickly to somebody else without grilling me on how much I had twisted the facts to get my effect. Now the truth can be told. It is, of course, a little more complicated than that woman will ever know.

One evening after work, I had taken a different route home just for variety's sake. On my way I noticed that a brick Tudor that we'd always admired was for sale. Curiosity being what it is, I jotted down the telephone number of the Realtor. At home I announced that the Tudor was on the market. We called the Realtor five minutes later to set up an appointment. We neglected to tell him that we were operating out of the idlest kind of curiosity and had no intention of buying anything.

The next day when we got inside the house, we thought it was cramped, ugly, and needed a lot of work. From the look on the Realtor's face, he seemed to agree. "If you have the time, there's a house nearby that may be more you," he said. Why not? we thought, we had seen one house already.

So, we entered the front door of the house that was more "us": the hardwood floors had been refinished; a fireplace dominated the living room; beveled glass doors led to the dining room; coved ceilings were accented with dark wood molding; a new deck stood outside the kitchen door. This two-bedroom 1926 bungalow was *it*. We bought the house on the spot. Accidents happen.

If I hadn't taken that particular different route, if I hadn't jotted down the phone number, if we had had something better to do than run around gawking at one house after another, all that followed would have been very different. Consider the chances of all these circumstances coming together like that and then answer this question: Was it *really* an accident?

When we walked our friends through the house before the sale closed and it was officially ours, they went silent as if they were holding their breaths. Obviously, they didn't see the potential we saw in it and were choosing to be discreet. We didn't care. We were so glad that all we as new owners would have to do was paint.

We set to work and didn't stop until the off-white walls were a distant memory. Since the bungalow was sited in such a way that not much sunlight came into its rooms to begin with, we went all out to make it a cozy cave. When those of little faith first set eyes on the cocoa-brown bedroom and the forest-green study, all they could say was, "Did you want it this dark?"

Winter nights we'd have the fireplace blazing, music blasting out of the sound system (it was Neil Young's *Trans* on vinyl for way longer than our friends could stand), and we were in heaven. More quickly than we had imagined, our circle got over the shock of the color scheme and the house became a refuge for us all.

Our honeymoon with the house was blissful until the reality hit that old houses are like bad knees: they require *constant* care. There we were, two novices, faced with things that needed to be attended to, right now, no excuses, today, or else: exploding light fixtures, mice in the attic, garage doors that jammed, flooding basements, temperamental appliances, vent fans that needed to be installed, the roof, you name it, the list was endless.

We had walked into this deal with all the confidence that we placed in accidents—we had met by accident six years before and that was good; we had bought the house because of a series of unduplicatable, apparently fortuitous, accidents; we had our delicious cake of a house almost handed to us. But here was the shadow to the dream: upkeep and repairs.

What we discovered for the first time about each other was that not only did we not like dealing with repairs, but any and all of these crises sent us each into a different kind of coma. Each time an old-house surprise bubbled up, we'd find ourselves having another nasty fight, something we never had in all those earlier years. We were just a mess as a problem-solving unit in this one crucial area. Sure, we'd tough our way through each house crisis, and we'd back off to recover. Then we'd live in dread of the next time. There was always a next time in that house. Welcome to where accidents will take you.

One of the ways we recovered from fights over repair crises was to work together on repainting a room. How many times can you repaint a room? Let us count the ways. We seemed to be painting all the time, in stages making each room darker and darker. To our way of thinking, the house was becoming more and more itself. Each shift down the color scale made it more beautiful to us.

During one of our regular painting jags, we decided to transform the dining room to a rich red. The fellow at the hardware store dutifully mixed the selection from the chip but shook his head while he did it. When I got the paint home and we tested it on the wall, it was way too tomato red for us. I took the can of paint back to have more black pigment added. The fellow said, "I've got to warn you that if this is too dark, we can't reverse it, you'll have to start over." He had no idea.

The darker mix was perfect, like Moroccan leather, with the color appearing to change depending on the light in the room. We loved it. One of the inevitable dissenters said it was the first dining room he had seen painted "Meatloaf." Everybody's a critic.

More than the color had changed in the dining room, though. In its shifting red guise, it seemed to have a remarkable new power: it pushed people to divulge secrets. Nobody was immune, not even my usually tight-lipped friend Diana. One Saturday over lunch she stopped talking about her vacation plans abruptly and, almost in a frenzy, dove into a long story about Jason, a man who had worked in her office and had irritated her to distraction for years.

Until this Saturday lunch, Diana had claimed that work was a dream since the day three months earlier that Jason left for a new job and was out of her life. But here Jason was, the topic of conversation once again. As Diana began to rant, I wondered if we can ever really be free of these monsters once they have insinuated their ways into our lives.

"Jason has a new boyfriend. Todd. Very nice," Diana said. "They seem devoted to one another."

"Jason is one lucky guy, isn't he?" I said.

That was not what Diana wanted to hear. She wanted me to say that Jason didn't deserve a new boyfriend who was nuts about him.

"I house-sat for them while they went off for a romantic getaway last week," she said. Pain was all over her face.

"You don't do this kind of thing," I said.

"No, I don't," she said. "Usually." There was a story here.

It seemed that Diana had developed an obsession about Jason and Todd's relationship as soon as Jason told her his good news. She was so certain that the ooey-gooey show they presented to her was a fraud that she was determined to find evidence that it was. And house-sitting for them let her roam free to uncover what she was sure was the sordid truth.

"So, Sherlock, what did you find?" I asked.

She gave me a look but couldn't stop herself. We were in the power of the dining room. "They leave little notes for each other. The notes say things like, 'I love you and you are a gift to me.' The notes are everywhere. A Teddy bear even has the note attached to it that it had when Todd gave it to Jason for their second-month anniversary. The second month!" Diana was losing it. I was thinking we should move to another room before something even worse came out.

"It must be simple happiness," I said.

"There is no such thing as simple happiness," she snapped,

Fifty years ago Gertrude Stein said that when people questioned her about her situation, with their implied need for her to apologize for her arrangement and explain away her contentment, she simply asked them if they were happy with what they had. That Saturday, I didn't remind Diana of Gertrude Stein's canny approach. I figured that she was already in deep enough shock that she had revealed she had become a spy in the house of love. By the way, that was the last time Diana mentioned Jason to me, and she never set foot in the dining room again.

Not long after Diana proclaimed that she didn't believe in simple happiness, or at least not for people she didn't like, we discovered that the wallpaper in the study was peeling and flaking.

When I checked the biggest piece hanging off the wall, I saw that it consisted of five or six layers virtually welded together and covered with sprayed-on texturing. The piece was so brittle that it snapped in my hand. There was no way that this piece could be glued back in place. Our beautiful forest-green walls that had held up so well for over eight years were crumbling. There was only one thing to be done: the walls of the study had to be stripped down to the original plaster.

One of our handy friends assured us that steaming wallpaper off is a snap. We believed him. We are so trusting. Of course, he didn't realize how the layers had been welded together over the course of sixty years. For five brutal and exhausting weeks, we spent every minute we weren't working or sleeping whittling the wallpaper free from the plaster. So much for the guarantees of knowledgeable friends.

When we finished the stripping, one look at the plaster walls told us that we couldn't simply paint the room. The walls were old, cracked, uneven. We could either texture the walls or go for the new experience of wallpaper. After five weeks trying to undo the results of texturing, we went for wallpaper. It took two weeks to locate a pattern we liked, and then in a marathon weekend, we put it up. When we finished we were in shock at how beautiful it was.

After we got over the transformation, we faced two hard facts. First, the wallpaper we had selected (to us it was the only real choice) was solid black with a minuscule fleur-de-lis pattern in dark blue. We had reached the farthest edge of the color spectrum. There was nowhere else to go. Second, we had managed to renovate the study without going at each other's throats. It had taken us nine years of hanging in there to get to this point of working as a team on projects that both of us would rather abandon than begin.

In the dining room, we sat down to celebrate a job well done by opening a bottle of wine. We had pulled off an incredible stunt. We had proved it to ourselves. We didn't need to prove it again. We had better things to do with our time. We said to each other, "Let's sell this place and move to something where we don't have to fix everything all the time." We were reclaiming pleasure.

And so we did. And though we had nine invaluable years in that house, the best thing we ever did together (that wasn't sex) was to sell it. I hope I never have to hold another plumber's wrench as long as I live. Chandler will never have to go up a ladder on to a roof again.

These days we live in a condo that requires zero maintenance. The rooms are uniformly white and we haven't lifted a paintbrush in eight years. Friends who grew to love our cozy color-mad bungalow are in shock at our new digs, so full of light. We've come to realize that we hardly ever cleaned the bungalow. Its darkness meant we could ignore the dirt piling up in the shadows.

Now we see everything clearly, can't ignore it, and we have to act. This is true too of our relationship. Our ever-deepening regard for each other and the way we spend time at home together remain the same: there's still the fire ablaze in the fireplace, music blasting out of the sound system (now Abbey Lincoln's *A Turtle's Dream* on CD), and as much laughter as ever. We still shudder at memories of those days of house repairs and wonder how we survived it and managed to grow from it.

In our new surroundings, we've gained something unexpected too: time. We can actually leave home without heading directly for the hardware store. Serendipity is alive and well out there and has welcomed us back. A few weeks ago, we were having drinks with three friends. Brian asked to try Marcia's drink, a Negroni. He took a sip and said, "It isn't as snappy as a whiskey sour."

"It's a Negroni. It's not supposed to be as snappy as a whiskey sour," Marcia replied. "Why don't you try it again without expectations?"

We all laughed. But here we were handed, in eight simple words, the absolute best advice anybody can offer another person. Whether it concerns a relationship, a friendship, a house, the color of a room, or a drink, stepping back for another look could do the trick. Maybe it won't be the right thing for you after all, but then again maybe the evidence will be clearer on the second look. The accidental universe still leaves us that choice.

Michael Greenspan

and Jesse Monteagudo

-four-

a jewish family

JESSE MONTEAGUDO AND MICHAEL GREENSPAN

JESSE

I met my lover at temple, thirteen years ago this February. As one of the lay leaders of Congregation Etz Chaim (CEC), Miami's gay and lesbian synagogue, I was conducting services that night. Throughout the services, I couldn't help but notice a handsome, husky, bearded man who was smiling at me. That man was Michael Greenspan, who approached me after services and began a relationship that is still going on. It was Michael's first time at Etz Chaim, and he almost didn't make it. Then as now a professional musician, Michael had to choose between Shabbat services at CEC and a performance of the Polish Dance Company, which was playing locally that night. Happily, he chose Etz Chaim.

MICHAEL

I had only recently come to terms with my orientation and had spent a number of months sampling the goodies. I was like a newborn adolescent discovering delights that I previously would not allow myself to consider. This secret shadow life was beginning to grow old because it really wasn't a part of my true nature. I wanted something more. I needed something more.

JESSE

It was not love at first sight, at least as far as I was concerned. I was then (1985) at the tail end of a nine-year, codependent relationship, and I wasn't in a mood for marriage. In fact, I admit in retrospect, I was planning to head for the baths after I left the synagogue. I was out of the closet since the early seventies, and an active member of South Florida's gay community for most of that time. Michael, on the other hand, had only recently come to terms with his homosexuality. I was a thirty-one-year-old Cuban-American who converted to Judaism as a young adult. Michael was a thirty-five-year-old Southern Jew, the grandson of Eastern European immigrants. We came together, at that moment in time, with different experiences and different aspirations.

MICHAEL

It is not that I planned to find a lover right there on the spot, but I knew that I was ready for the next step in my coming-out process—making real friends within the community and hoping eventually to establish a permanent relationship. My involvement with the Jewish community had always been strong. After discovering the existence of a synagogue for gay and lesbian Jews in my own city, I was excited about finding my niche there.

JESSE

My relations with Michael got no further than the conversation stage that night. Michael went off with a group of congregants to an all-night deli, and I went to the baths. The following Friday night, Michael tells me, he returned to the synagogue, but I wasn't there: I was in Orlando attending a leather club run. I returned to services the following week and met Michael, still waiting for me and hoping to pick up where we left off two weeks earlier. That's when I remembered what attracted me in the first place: Michael's wit, his curiosity, his rich, dark beard, his bright eyes, and his bewitching smile. We went to a local club, but only for a while. Michael invited me to go home with him, and the rest is history.

MICHAEL

Jesse and I looked at each other during the service which he led. His smile melted me and his soft brown eyes seemed to invite me to approach him during the social hour that followed the service. But I was still shy about these things.

Inviting him home seemed like the wrong move under the circumstances. I wanted to know him for real. A friendly group of congregants invited me to go out to a local deli for a late supper that evening. Jesse declined the invitation to join us, and I lost my opportunity. It was two weeks later that I saw him at services again. I wasn't going to make the same mistake twice!

JESSE

Although I did not want to start a new relationship at that time, Michael would not take "no" for an answer. As winter turned into spring, Michael went from being one of many to being the main one to being the only one. We became officially an item during the first weekend in May, which was also my birthday and Congregation Etz Chaim's anniversary weekend. In August, I moved out of the North Broward house that I shared with my ex— with whom I still lived—and joined Michael in an apartment in Fort Lauderdale. Michael and I lived in that apartment until 1992, when we moved into a condominium home in Plantation, a suburb west of Fort Lauderdale. It was the gay suburban dream come true.

MICHAEL

I was in love from the start. Jesse was well connected within the community as a writer and activist. He taught me about our history, struggles, and triumphs. He introduced me to the people who had been important to our community. I learned and I loved him. I never was more determined to win his heart.

JESSE

In a sense, it is appropriate that we met at a CEC service and cemented our relationship at the synagogue's anniversary party. To a great extent, our thirteen-year union has been a three-way relationship, with Etz Chaim as the third party. I have served on the CEC board, on and off, since 1978; and in 1986 Michael was elected president of the congregation; he moved up fast. Michael served as president until 1988; after a year's hiatus, I was elected president and served until 1991. This year, after several years as song leader and chair of the ritual committee, Michael will complete his second term as CEC president. Although he and I are active in other clubs and organizations, Etz Chaim remains number one.

Indeed, Michael and I are just your typical southern Florida, suburban Jewish couple, only gay and without children. A few years ago, we applied for membership at the local Jewish Community Center (JCC), which has, among other things, an excellent gym. The "J" was happy to sell us two individual memberships, but we opted for the family membership, which was cheaper. As the first queer couple to request a family membership, we caused an uproar at that JCC, although the issue was old hat elsewhere. Finally, after much soul-searching and a few phone calls, we were offered a family membership. It was, in a sense, a victory for the cause, and other same-sex couples later walked through the door that we opened.

If joining the JCC as a couple was a small step forward for the movement, so was our move to Raintree Forest Condominium. The unit was near-perfect, the surroundings were ideal, it was located halfway between our respective jobs, and it was a vast improvement over the rental apartment that we had called home. Although we never made a public announcement of our sexual orientation, we hung a rainbow flag from our window—so visitors could find us—and we are obviously a couple. Still, the screening committee accepted us with open arms, and the condo community's reaction to our presence has been largely positive, if only because we don't drink, we don't make noise, and we do our best to make our community a nice place to live. In fact, they liked us so much that they elected me to the board of the condo association barely a month after we moved in. I served for two years, after which time Michael was elected to the same position (secretary) that I occupied between 1992 and 1994.

Judaism is a group religion, and Jewish holidays and life-cycle events center around the family. Our relationship with my biological family is strained at best, but I was welcomed by Michael's family with open arms. Each year we travel to Greensboro, North Carolina, to join Michael's family for the Passover Seder. In a sense, Michael's family is the Jewish family I never had, a role also played by Congregation Etz Chaim.

MICHAEL

My family has been supportive of my disclosure from the very beginning. After I came to terms with myself, I had no trouble sharing this information with both friends and family. I count myself as being one of the luckiest people to have been able to take such support for granted. When Jesse and I were beginning our relationship, my family accepted him as part of the family. They were already pleased that I had taken the first step at checking out the gay synagogue. In fact, it was my mother who convinced me to forgo the Polish Dance Company that first night, and go to Etz Chaim. That Jesse is a part of my family is obvious; both my mother's and father's sides love and accept him totally.

JESSE

Michael Greenspan is my lover, my best friend, and my soul mate. We share a lot in common: music, the theater, chocolate, nature walks, stuffed animals, the Blue Ridge Parkway, liberal politics, leather and bear clubs, and, of course, Congregation Etz Chaim. Sometimes I wonder how he puts up with me, but I am glad that he does. We hope to be together until it's time to go, together or apart.

MICHAEL

Jesse Monteagudo is my lover, my best friend, and my soul mate. Neither one of us is perfect, but our relationship is based on mutual love, respect, and care. I love doing anything with Jesse. Life's road is full of twists, turns, and surprises, but that is okay because with God's will, we hope to travel that road together for many, many years to come.

It's not complicated:

I WANT TO MARRY THE MAN I LOVE.

Case closed!

David Pandozzi and David Yegerlehner

-five-

two husbands named david

DAVID PANDOZZI AND DAVID YEGERLEHNER

We get a lot of mileage out of having the same first name. We usually carry a sign in the Gay Pride Parade, "David & David, Together for . . ." however many years it is that year; the cheers are louder and the smiles a bit broader because of our names, and sometimes because we dress identically for the occasion. We've been called Davids Doubled, Davids Squared, and people tend to remember our names when we're introduced at a party or a meeting. "Two for the price of one," we sometimes hear, and our return address labels read "The Davids." Only once have we suspected less than ideal results: one of our much-traveled friends, who is not out to his parents, sometimes stays at our apartment on trips to New York. He told his folks many years ago that he stays with the Davids on his visits here, and to this day they assume that we are a straight couple, Mr. and Mrs. David.

Since one of us is a head taller than the other, we have always been known as Big David and Little David (never Tall David and Short David).

In our fifth year together (1982) we bought wedding bands. There was no wedding, but we realized by that point that we were a match, with a fairly healthy chance of making a permanent go of it. Not that we wore our rings to make a broadcast to the world—in the early

1980s we were not as out as we are today—but this was a valentine to ourselves. We liked the rings because they were a symbol that we had found each other: in the words of the wedding vows, the outward and visible sign of the inward and spiritual grace that we felt. As time went on, however, the rings did become a proclamation, a defiance—and facilitated outing ourselves. In 1996 a new colleague asked Big David, "What does your wife do?"

"I don't have a wife."

"But I see your wedding ring."

"That's because I have a husband."

We're not satisfied with any of the terms: lover, companion, friend, spouse, husband . . . but husband is our label of choice because its meaning is unequivocal. We want the people we rub shoulders with everyday to know that we are related by marriage as much as if we were a straight couple. It would now be an outrage to accept the long-standing verdict of the straight world that our marriage should never be spoken of openly. What straight woman would go along with the idea that she should keep it a secret that the guy who calls her daily at the office is her husband? Four years after buying the wedding bands, we bought signet rings bearing interlocking D's. We wear our rings as an outward and visible sign that we are a unit worthy of public acknowledgment.

Analyzing a twenty-year love affair—figuring out what makes it work—may seem to be a daunting task. But twenty years of shared days, about 7,000 of them so far, provide a lot of data. Novelist Christopher Bram, reflecting on seventeen years with his companion, confesses that he is "surprised at the life we've made together, how we both feel better grounded in this thicker, heavier, shared experience." There are many elements that make a life together substantial, making it subject more to gravitational than to centrifugal forces: we came out at the same time and at about the same age (early thirties), we were very serious about wanting stability, we liked each other, we had similar passions in life, and we had two children to take part in raising, a girl and a boy from Big David's ten-year heterosexual marriage.

Big David caught Little David on the rebound and on the move, off to New York City from Providence, Rhode Island, to fulfill a lifelong yearning to be near the Broadway theater, not as an actor, but as a connoisseur. Our dating had been under way for a year or so as Little David was falling out of love with someone else, and we decided to give New York a try together, since we had both been eyeing it for years, although for different reasons. Little David couldn't get enough of Broadway; since his late teens he had made weekend forays from Providence to New York, seeing three or four shows in two days. Big David had fantasized about a Manhattan sabbatical for years; he had once heard a woman claim that she had visited the Metropolitan Museum of Art every week for a year and had yet to see it all; what a draw that was. And his earliest memories from childhood in Indiana included hearing the Saturday afternoon Metropolitan Opera broadcasts. Big David was in Worcester, Massachusetts, about an hour's drive from Little David in Providence. New York was where we both wanted to be; as we dated and discovered our mutual longings, we decided not to resist the lure of New York.

But Manhattan is not a cultural theme park. New York is Broadway, museums, and opera, but it's a hard place to establish footing and survive. The first reality check was finding an apartment. With $3,000 in borrowed money and a naiveté that probably served us well, we trudged from one apartment building to another looking for a vacancy, working from a list of available apartments purchased for forty-five dollars from one of the sleazy apartment agencies that existed in those days. We saw many apartments that anyone west of the Hudson would have considered walk-in closets. But we finally found a newly renovated one-bedroom with a real kitchen, and the elderly landlord who had turned away others decided that we looked trustworthy enough (we'd had the sense to wear suits and ties). We ended up with the apartment that turned out to be our home for the next eighteen years.

As a matter of fact, we had ended up with a deal; the apartment, on the Upper East Side of Manhattan, was rent stabilized at $350 a month. Later, near the end of our first lease, shopping around for other space, we found how much of a deal we had. For a fraction of what we would have to pay in rent elsewhere, we could make our little place look great. So these two New York newlyweds put our energies into our apartment, our city, and our kids.

But first, with all our possessions barely inside the door, a jumble of boxes and cartons (one U-Haul truck from Worcester, another from Providence), Little David left on a Florida vacation that had been planned for months—with cousins and nieces and nephews. So while he was getting his fill of the Magic Kingdom, Big David had more than a week to try to put everything into order. Anyone who remembers how Jane Fonda transformed the apartment in *Barefoot in the Park* will get the idea. It does happen in real life: Little David came back to the apartment and found it transformed into a home; he arrived back on May 18, which we mark as our anniversary.

To say that the apartment was minimalist is an understatement. The TV was a small black and white portable—no cable, no antenna, and barely any picture; the bookshelves were boards on cinder blocks. The couch was a cardboard-staples-polyester item picked up when Big David was trying to put together a life after divorce; the dining table was a hand-me-down from his childhood in Indiana. There was no bed: just a mattress and box springs on the floor. Half of the floor (the kitchen and dining areas) was covered with hideous red indoor-outdoor carpeting installed during the renovation. Little by little, as our finances improved over the years, part of the joy we shared derived from making our apartment into space that was satisfying and comfortable, and a reflection of us. By the twelfth year, literally everything within the four walls had changed, the floors, the walls themselves, even the ceiling. Our tastes coincided remarkably well, and there were no huge disagreements as we shopped for carpets or wallpaper, the bed and couch. We created a haven for ourselves, just large enough for ourselves, a resting place from a city that held our attention.

In the early years there was lingering paranoia that it wouldn't last, that we might split up. There were the occasional panic attacks, one of us embracing the other tightly, pleading, Please don't leave me, not brought on by anything in particular, just insecurity and a horror of being parted from someone who had become so much a part of oneself. Maybe such paranoia visits straight marriages too, but probably not with the same intensity. For two men not legally bound, the coupling process seems more fragile. Supposedly divorce is harder for straights because legal disentangling is involved.

But bit by bit separation had become unthinkable. One of our friends accused us of being joined at the hip, and we didn't mind at all. We enjoyed that order of things, the regularity, the pattern. There was order in our universe, and we brought order to the universe. Because we were joined at the hip, some of our friends have said, "Please, you guys, never split up—you give us hope." We even sleep on the same sides of the bed, always, something we didn't even realize was noticed. One night, on a whim, we switched sides. It happened on a night that our son Josiah was driving in late from Massachusetts; he had keys to the apartment and let himself in. We were already in bed reading; Josiah came into the bedroom to bring us up-to-date on news. After a couple of minutes, he stopped in mid-sentence and looked over at us: "You guys have switched sides."

We were serious about stability, we wanted a healthy marriage. As two men in our thirties intent on absorbing New York, we were not interested in turmoil, and we had no desire to revisit the dating game. The unspoken contract almost from the beginning was that we would be true to each other; we sensed that extramarital affairs would be too bruising. Obviously when AIDS entered the picture in the early 1980s, there was a very practical reason for monogamy. But for us the very practical reason for monogamy was that we didn't want to hurt each other emotionally or physically.

Intimacy—connecting at a level that really knits two people together—is hard enough to achieve as it is, much harder to come by than sexual performance. We wouldn't trade what we were building for the "freedom" to mess around for the fun of it. Part of it, to be sure, is that we are very traditional. We both came from environments in which marriage means fidelity, and having hyper-concern for the feelings and well-being of the other. We were not interested in reinventing or "improving" on this concept. But believe it or not, as much fun as sex is—and not because our interest in sex has diminished—we made the discovery that, sometimes, just holding one another can be the most important form of making love. In the film *A Man of No Importance*, Albert Finney's lifelong straight buddy, an elderly widower, confesses that what he misses the most about married life is "the cuddling." Sometimes in the middle of the day we just lie on the bed, fully clothed, holding each other for twenty or thirty minutes; every night we fall asleep in each other's arms whether we've had sex or not.

Now the reality of living together—love working itself out in the give-and-take of the daily routine—has led us to resent the word "homosexual," primarily because it is one-dimensional, and that's not life. We suspect that the word "homosexual" was invented by a straight man, unlucky in love, who decided, for whatever reason, to study why it is that men get it on. The study was too narrowly focused. Homo*sex*ual—sex right there in the middle claiming center stage. No one who has really been in love, who has succeeded in making a happy life together with another person, would claim sex as the foundation. Often the people who want to appear broadminded say, "It doesn't make any difference to me whom you sleep with," as if that were the essence of either homosexuality or heterosexuality.

What you do besides the sex is what matters most. John Klomp got it right in his essay in the *Harvard Gay and Lesbian Review* critiquing *The Bath* (painting) and *Bath II* (photo): "Why should it matter to society whom you get out of bed with in the morning and shave and shower with before going off to work?" Get out of bed with, not go to bed with! That turns the conventional positioning of things on its head, and rightly so. The reality is that, no matter if a couple is straight or gay, most attention has to be paid to the business of living. Even if you spend an hour every day having sex, every day without fail, that's still only 4 percent of your life. If you're not connecting in a multitude of other ways, there's not enough to sustain a marriage.

It became unimaginable that our keenest interests and key experiences would not be shared; we saw from the beginning the rewards of being a couple. Seeing the joy of the other person as we made discoveries together was more than half the fun. And we each had life experiences to tap into to make life more interesting for the other. Big David had no idea that you could sneak into Broadway theaters: the time-honored tradition in theater circles of "second acting." During intermission when people come outside for a smoke or fresh air, you mingle with the crowd and then, as casually as possible, stroll into the theater. Little David had mastered this strategy over the years, and Big David was terrified the first time he went along—but that night we got to see Liza Minnelli in *The Act*. Of course, it doesn't work if the house is sold out, or if it's raining, and there's not much point if all the hit songs are in the first act, unless of course, it's Liza on stage, or Carol Channing, or Christopher Plummer. We've seen a lot of great theater that we would otherwise have missed.

But when times were flush, we paid full fare. Big David bought tickets for *Nicholas Nickleby*—$100 per ticket, six hours of theater—without even telling Little David, and on the Saturday of the performance told him, "Follow me." How much more it all has meant because we were sitting holding hands, laughing together, crying together, for such theater experiences as *Angels in America, La Cage aux Folles, Sweeney Todd, She Loves Me, The King and I, My Fair Lady, Les Misérables, Cats, Love! Valour! Compassion!*, Liza at Carnegie Hall, *Follies* in concert at Avery Fisher Hall, and *A Chorus Line*, to name but a few. We've attended several Tony Awards ceremonies, and made a stab at all thirty-six Shakespeare plays; we bought subscriptions to the Public Theatre Shakespeare Marathon (stretched out over about six years) and managed to see most of them.

But up Broadway about twenty blocks from the theater district is the Metropolitan Opera. Big David had barely heard of Stephen Sondheim before we became a couple, and Little David had almost no acquaintance with Wagner, or the fine art of really getting into an opera. Opera is not an easily accessible art form, and many people pass it by because they aren't willing to work at it. But Big David found in Little David a rare kindred spirit, someone who was willing to work at it. *Tosca* means a lot to us because, when we were dating, we sat arm in arm in Big David's Worcester apartment listening to *Tosca* from beginning to end and following the libretto word for word. One of our first New York events together was hearing *Tosca* from box seats at the Met. Years later we gave the same treatment to the four operas of Wagner's *Ring*. Little David had grown up on Sondheim, Big David had grown up on Wagner, and our relationship was enriched because we were each willing to follow the other's lead.

Sometimes a life together can be enhanced by factors that could never have been anticipated or predicted. For example, when we got together, who could have known that we would purchase our gold and diamond wedding bands at a shop in Port Elizabeth, South Africa?

Not long after we moved in together in 1978, Big David showed Little David a small bundle of letters, the earliest of which dated from 1961. The carefully preserved letters were from Big David's pen pal, David Watson, in Port Elizabeth. The correspondence had begun when Big David was in college and had continued until his coming out and divorce in 1974–75—there was not much about those events he felt like telling a straight pen pal on the other side of the world. But life was settled now, and Little David urged that the correspondence be resumed.

Our letter to David Watson brought a prompt response; he was pleased to once again have word of David in America. Of course, we had not told him the whole story—just that we had moved to New York together, shared an apartment, had found jobs, were excited about being so close to Broadway. What more did he need to know? Nothing, as it turns out. Watson read between the lines and delivered a bit of news that he had never even hinted at during the first thirteen years of correspondence: for all of those years he had been living with Ben—something he had not felt like telling a straight pen pal on the other side of the world. Now we really had a lot to tell each other, so much so that we soon began corresponding by audiotape. It was one of the high points of the month to come home and find a tape in the mailbox; for sixty or ninety minutes we would snuggle on the couch or lie on the bed together and listen to David and Ben. And we would prepare a tape in response, describing our New York adventures or bringing them up-to-date on what was happening with the kids.

Well over a year before Big David's fortieth birthday, we decided to ease the pain of that occasion by going to South Africa to meet David and Ben. We planned Port Elizabeth as the final destination, with stops first at Victoria Falls in Zimbabwe, Johannesburg, and Cape Town. From their end, David and Ben arranged for us to be met by gay friends at every stop along the way. One of our most memorable evenings of the trip was a dinner party held in our honor—we were total strangers—by a dozen gay men in Harare, Zimbabwe. Yes, we are everywhere!

But how do you plan the first meeting of men who had been pen pals for over twenty years? What is appropriate for such an occasion? As it turned out, events fell into place as if planned by a great Hollywood director. David and David had invited David and Ben to join us riding the famed Blue Train from Johannesburg to Cape Town; they had declined, but David Watson agreed to meet us in Cape Town, to tour there, and then drive us all to Port Elizabeth. The Blue Train ride takes twenty-four hours, noon to noon, exactly; the engineer will actually slow the train down if it's ahead of schedule. David Watson was waiting on the platform as the train pulled into Cape Town. There it was that three old new friends embraced for the first time. We checked into the grand old lady of Cape Town hotels, the Mount Nelson, sharing a magnificent suite: a huge living room with David Watson's bedroom on one side, ours on the other. On the morning of Big David's fortieth birthday, we awoke to the awesome view of Table Mountain from our bedroom window. David Watson introduced us to a retired diplomat, Ian Den, who had once danced with the Queen of England in Rhodesia; Ian gave us a two-day tour of the Cape Town region before Watson drove us to Port Elizabeth to meet Ben and spend a week in their home. It was during that week that we bought our wedding bands at a shop on Main Street. We had pulled off this trip together, we were with another gay couple who had helped us fashion memories of a lifetime. We felt closer than ever before.

We would make one more trip to South Africa. Early in 1986 we received a late-night call from David Watson that Ben had died suddenly of a heart attack. In December of that year, to be with our friend for the holidays, we flew directly to Port Elizabeth for a two-week stay. A few years later we saw David Watson again. We assured him that, although we loved him very much, we couldn't travel to South Africa again. It was too far away, and we wanted to see the rest of the world. The compromise was to meet in Europe: the three Davids rented a car and toured Spain and Portugal together. David Watson is retired now and on a limited pension. But he has a handsome young boyfriend and still dreams of the day when he will walk down Broadway with David and David. Our life as a couple has been enriched beyond measure because the other David has been along for the ride.

Although we have managed international travel from time to time (we've also been to London, Paris, and Mexico), most of our travel was much closer to home: the kids, Deborah and Josiah, lived with their mother in Worcester, and for many years we made a monthly drive to Massachusetts to spend weekends with them. Was Big David lucky enough to find in Little David a man who loved children, yearning to be a father himself? No. But it was enough that he found someone who liked *these* kids, and took the responsibilities of parenting with utmost seriousness. Little David has said many times over the years that one of the scariest things about getting involved with Big David was that kids were part of the deal. As if it weren't scary enough that he was moving in with another person, for all practical purposes, for the first time "getting married and settling down." Even sharing, however tangentially, a parenting role had never even been contemplated when Little David was looking for Mr. Right; kids, even kids 200 miles away, factored into the relationship big-time. But he knew, and accepted, that these children—Deb was ten, Si was seven—were now part of his life too. It didn't hurt, obviously, that they were good kids.

Hence it was just a given that Big David would never go to Worcester by himself; we always saw the kids together. It was a given as well that the monthly child support payments could never be missed. As much as Little David had a reputation for "not liking kids," that was for kids in the abstract, or for kids who were a pain in the ass, which Deb and Si were not. And Little David came to see the kids not just as responsibility, but as opportunity as well. Although most of the time we drove to Worcester, a few times a year they came to visit us in New York. Now, one of Little David's role models in life has been Auntie Mame. He's been the primary entertainment coordinator in the family—"life is a banquet and you should live, live, live." As far as the kids were concerned, Manhattan was the ultimate cultural theme park, and Little David wanted to make sure they didn't miss it. By the time the kids were in their mid-teens, they had already seen and done more in Manhattan than the average American school kid could have done on a dozen class trips to the big city.

Deb is now twenty-nine and lives with her husband, Dennis, in California; Si is twenty-six and lives with his wife, Elena, near Boston. For eighteen years they visited us in our small apartment in Manhattan, and they brought their future spouses there to meet us. We know the very date that we first met Elena (March 12, 1993) because our New York City Domestic Partnership Certificate had been acquired that day and was on the dining table. Si had gone with us to get the certificate, and because he handed over the dollar to the notary public, likes to claim that he paid for our wedding. Elena saw the certificate on the table—Si had told her that our trip to city hall had been the main errand for the day—and congratulated us warmly. Both kids managed to find spouses who had no problem with a father-in-law who was married to a man. When Deb brought Dennis home for the first time, we enjoyed marathon discussions about gay marriage. On Gay Pride Day observing Stonewall 25 in 1994, Si and Elena joined us (along with a few thousand others) carrying the mile-long rainbow flag up Manhattan's First Avenue.

Curiously enough, our being gay was never openly discussed with the kids until late in the game, until they were adults, mainly because of Big David's insecurity on the matter. Kids don't come out to their parents because they're scared to: it works in the other direction as well. We officially "outed" ourselves to the kids by sending them an article about us in a gay magazine.

For our kids, we suppose, gay marriage needs no defense or explanation. They've seen it lived for years, and it's no different from straight marriage. No doubt it took a while for them to realize that papa and David were married, but we were such a unit, and after a point, two men together becomes old news. When Deb was perhaps eleven or twelve, on one of our weekend trips to Worcester, we all had stayed in one room at a Marriott. She reported one morning that she'd seen something funny, and she was giggling as she told us: "Papa, when you were sleeping this morning, you had your arm around David." As she grew older she realized that two men *loving* one another overrode the significance of two *men* loving one another. At Si's wedding, when I asked her if I should wear a pink triangle pin in my tuxedo lapel, she said, "Go for it."

We've described being together a lot, doing almost everything as a couple, so much so that friends have commented that we're joined at the hip. But for all that, many friends over the years have also noted how different we are; in many ways we are not alike at all. We wonder if we would have come up as a match at a computer dating service. But the points of connection are what matter, and sometimes these are not even immediately obvious; it takes a while for them to surface. Dating is discovering. So it's risky, even self-defeating, for people to shop for a mate with a list of must haves. Some of that has to be, naturally. But you might be surprised by who Mr. Right turns out to be. Marian the librarian in *The Music Man* tells her mother that she has her standards where men are concerned. Mother has no patience: "I know all about your standards, and if you don't mind my saying so, there's not a man alive who could hope to measure up to that blend of Paul Bunyan, St. Pat and Noah Webster you've concocted for yourself out of your Irish imagination, your Iowa stubbornness, and your library full of books." Yes, the romantic ideal. Who isn't tempted to believe that it's what we're all after? But the guy you're dreaming about, imagining through a soft-focus lens—and perhaps hoping will look like something out of *International Male*—is the guy who will have to help you with the laundry, and who may have a dozen habits that drive you up the wall. Many years ago we heard a woman say to her husband, "My dear, it's a good thing I love you as much as I do, because there are times when I really hate you." We are very different people, but there are so many points of deep connection and satisfaction to override those occasions when we annoy the hell out of each another. Having someone to share the journey with makes it all worthwhile.

To this day, we hold hands in the movies or at the theater, we kiss each other goodbye when one of us leaves the house, sometimes even on the street. For years our daily routines called for Big David to be up and out the door before Little David had to get out of bed. But before leaving the house Big David awoke Little David with a kiss and put his cup of tea on the bedside table. Sometimes Big David will stand behind Little David and rest his chin on his head as we look at a painting in a museum or wait for a bus. And we always fall asleep at night holding each other.

We never refer to ourselves any more as "lovers"; it sounds too extramarital, in the same class as "mistress." "Partners" could mean we're in business together. "Companion" is popular, and we sometimes use it, but it sounds too much like the person who stayed with Aunt

Edna during her declining years. "Spouse" might be forced into service sometimes, but who really uses "spouse" in everyday conversation? "Better half" is too flippant, "significant other" is too unwieldy, "life mate" too contrived. "Friend" or "roommate"? Well, we're not in a college dorm, and what married person says, "My roommate is picking me up after work"? And all of these terms are not gender specific: they are still a way of hiding.

Bruce Bawer has pointed out that "in the war against homophobia, a million gays marching on Washington would have less impact than a million gays being honest about their homosexuality in their respective homes and workplaces and houses of worship." So we commonly refer to one another as "husband," because it leaves no doubt that David is married to a man.

Allan Shore

and Stephen Corpus

- six -

long-term young love

A L L A N   D .   S H O R E

Often the picture of long-term committed gay or lesbian love is of an older couple that met in their adult years and formed a lasting, inspirational relationship. In this way positive, mature love is brought forth and placed upon a pedestal to be emulated, in much the same way that opposite-gender unions are dreamed as youthfully blissful and destined forever, starting young and growing effortlessly better.

For gay love, however, it is as if we leave out the process of the growing of the union, of the making of something special out of the unguided, unfocused, and confused reality of dreams meant to be whatever they become. And perhaps we miss out on some of the silliness of the development of caring.

My Stephen died one week after our eleventh anniversary. He was thirty-four and I thirty-seven, and we had a unique journey through a youthful long-term relationship. He was diagnosed about seven years into our togetherness, giving us only four years to factor in a much too predictable ending.

In retrospect, I believe ours was, in fact, an adult kind of youthful relationship. He and I learned and lived and cared within the limits of a dream that would not, could not last forever—at least not in body. No matter how hard we tried, we would miss out on the idealized wonder of the glory of mature love. But the dream was still there: present, visible, pulling, sometimes pushing.

Stephen never gave up his dream of a life whose control was at his fingertips, a dream driven by the immediacy of whatever happened in the time we were together. He went to his death crying and struggling to stay alive because he did not want me to be alone in the winter that had set in, as if the cold of those few days meant anything of real importance. Yet I know he knew better. Just days before, during one of his increasingly less frequent periods of coherency, he reminded me of his ending mantra: "I wish I could have met you before so today wouldn't have to be our future."

By "before" he meant, of course, before his infection, which we figured must have happened just days or weeks in advance of our introduction in 1984. I think he knew who gave it to him, although he would never name anyone, preferring to hint around. I don't think this secrecy had much to do with sparing me, but sprang more from the fact that his four sisters, parents, and in-laws knew these other couple of guys. They were not just passing experiences for Stephen; they were potential living connections to his "real" family, a near collision of realities, complex interactions of choice, culture (Filipino and white), and in a strange and terrifying way, blood relationships, as would clearly have been discovered had Stephen developed a relationship with one of the men who most likely infected him.

I sometimes imagine what life would have been like had it been I who infected him. But we who remain—me and my commingled family and maybe the others touched by Stephen's sexuality—have yet to explore this fact and its implications in that it may not have anything to do with who Stephen was or who we were to become.

Stephen and I met on New Year's Eve at the Bench and Bar, a downtown club in Oakland, California. He was standing, beautiful and gullible, next to the fireplace, in the days when it was actually used. The weather was cold, the flames warming. There weren't many people in the club yet. It was too early and people seldom came out until the need became more demanding; except me, of course, who nearly always got there ahead of convention. I was sitting at a table reading a political newspaper, of all things.

He would eventually grow to despise politics, claiming that it took too much of my time. I suspect he also knew that I used it as a diversion, compensating for my inability to speak with anything but a barren soul and pathetic honesty, something of which at the time he could not even conceive. This was obvious to Stephen, since I obviously didn't care what others thought of my reading about politics in a place where image meant much. And I could tell that Stephen had many secrets he did not want to share. Although he apparently cherished making and keeping them. He even seemed to enjoy lying, something that would eventually become a necessity to maintain pervasive, life-defining images. He liked the attention and his own ability to define the world in a way he thought useful at any particular moment.

He didn't lie on the night we met. He even told me right away, without regard to my feelings or those of my cockroaches, that he hated my apartment. The neighborhood was admittedly not particularly good, not really bad. To be either would give it more importance than it deserved. Stephen took my living in "that place," in Oakland, as one of the signs of my insistence on not taking enough credit for who I was and what I did in life. It was this, I think, that led us to talking a lot that first night. I knew that I talked more than I should have, partly due to the wine, partly due to the excitement of being with a young Asian man who laughed a lot as he met a dreamer of a white guy who talked to excess. We sat on the floor and told each other little snippets of things that seemed to bring us together and that we later learned would keep us going through the hard times. Looking back, it was almost as if we knew from the first moments that a temporal future was not ours to be: we worked so hard that night to make order of strange pieces.

When we finally got tired and went to bed, sleep came quickly. We arose gently in the morning and got ready for work. He told me as we were leaving the apartment how excited he was about meeting someone who didn't just want sex; we didn't have sex that night, and as I recall, I barely even thought of it. The eroticism came from the sense of instant connection; good, we knew, and solid.

I knew at once too that our being together brought up thoughts of love that scared him terribly. I think now of the fear being related to an internal knowledge that he was infected, ashamed as he felt about what he "had to do" in life to find the right person. He tried many times to speak of the fear of missing anything in life whenever he had signs of the tiniest of illnesses or physical discomforts. I discouraged him from focusing on this, thinking that his concerns arose from severe insecurity. I suspected, in fact, that his refusal to go to doctors for almost any reason heightened his sensitivity to pain. And I was very afraid of letting him play out what I thought was but one of his fantasies of worthlessness.

Fantasies drove his life: good ones and unusual ones. For work, for fun, for family, for love: he made up partial truths and thought only about how he could convert any situation into the best thing possible, for him in the early years, for us in the later. It was only later, in fact, after he discovered that I knew what he was doing, that he would begin using my knowledge of his style to try to outmaneuver me, or sometimes to make fun of the fact that I knew what he was doing. Other people—even those he knew well—would listen to and enjoy his twists and turns with life's events, yet still convey approving fascination with his revisionism. But like me they knew that something wasn't right about his stories. Still we let them go unchallenged, conspiracies that molded well with the best dreams everyone seemed to want for him.

Part of this power came from his being attractive, professional, and dapper. He and his world offered the best of everything, as he saw it, giving everyone the feeling not only that he possessed the elements of his imagination but also that those who questioned his view were lacking the capacity for sophisticated fun. So what's a little purified truthfulness?

In our early years, we had a lot of uncomfortable arguments. Stephen often took my passiveness, particularly around personal matters, as a sign that I was not interested in his need for control. Just the opposite I now know was (and is) true. I would rather have had him learn a lesson than spell out what I thought he should be learning. My partial awareness of this trait always made me concerned about making Stephen feel ignorant; it was evident that feeling this way made Stephen extremely uncomfortable, and sometimes angry. So when he wanted something to happen his way, I would give his concern a half-assed acknowledgment and follow up, calculatingly, with a question or two, an option maybe, to check and see if he could figure out a different possibility. Regardless of what conclusion he came to, I would then leave the issue alone, letting him go with whichever result made sense to him, hoping for him to learn. The funny thing was that he took my style as condescending, conveying exactly the message of ignorance that he most feared. He hated it. But rather than confront my approach, we just let these situations play out, appropriately or inappropriately, and nearly always uncomfortably for our entire time together. Only much later did I realize that he needed, wanted, demanded, craved for me to tell him to stop and aim him in another direction. I think that I finally internalized this in about year ten, when it was nearly irrelevant because he was slipping into death. Perhaps it was this unsettled give-and-take that made it best for us to travel in the company of others.

Stephen was a concierge at the St. Francis Hotel in San Francisco, a job requiring that he learn a good deal about a lot of places. At first we traveled mostly to the Napa Valley, Carmel Valley, the Monterey Peninsula—local visiting meccas. We have pictures of one beautiful early trip through the wine country and Pebble Beach in the company and elegance of a fully decked-out limo driver and superstretch, courtesy of one company or another that wanted Stephen's undying professional attention. This particular trip came, as usual, with numerous invites to fancy food and drink, word apparently out that a new player was on the professional field. Stephen was uncomfortable with this initial attention. I, on the other hand, relished the possibilities, stealing the little bottles of alcohol from the hotel refrigerators, knowing management would not even bother to charge the expenses to our bill. I took advantage of each offer of a free meal and pocketed some of the gift certificates he should have provided as incentives to his guests when he got back to work. (One of the benefits of not being married was that my relationship to the concierge was ambiguous, to say the least!) Stephen was embarrassed. And from that point on we traveled nearly everywhere with an entourage of family or friends. Stephen always insisted that the reason was to share the wealth of experiences. I suspect alternative intentions.

I definitely know that he learned right away that I would be less romantic when others were around. I never thought that I could be in a relationship with someone who was so afraid of affection and, as it would turn out, life in general. Even though I, like many people, have all kinds of visceral reactions to the thought of public affection with a gender kin, I nevertheless got over it quickly with a little encouragement (alcohol or otherwise). Stephen manipulated that encouragement.

Having others around was the easiest form of discouragement. Even in decidedly gay locations, the presence of others made a tremendous difference in the degree of acceptable connectedness. Of course, having biological family members around was the ultimate in emotional turnoffs. I hated this from the get-go because it was such a transparent form of closetedness. But I soon learned that it may well have been the fertilizer for our longevity. No matter how uncomfortable the family of "others" was or wasn't about outright affection, any witness to togetherness was an obvious road map to emotional vulnerabilities and undoubtedly "neon-ized" the existence of his life of fantasies. But some of the fun with these games kept life interesting, even when the truth was overt.

Competition with his sisters was an element of his insistence on disguising the truth, deception being so easily mixed in with his games of skill. He liked a great deal to have the best and the most timely goodies. He did this a lot by "borrowing" money and things (the concept of paying back being a bit foreign) from his family and a few others and then finding interesting ways to twist ownership. One of his sisters liked this game, too, although she would doubt it, reinforcing at the time the emotional choreography and upping the ante to succeed. Together and separately they got quite good at this sport.

When I wrote his obituary, which turned out not to be used for a variety of troublesome logistical reasons, I said that Stephen died from complications related to AIDS and from too many fears. Neither the newspaper nor any of his eulogizers—myself included—acknowledged the line at the time. Perhaps none of us understood what it meant; and, of course, it did not comply with conventionality, a critical component of successful grieving in some families. I prefer to believe that the reasons are quite different: that people don't want to contemplate that someone they liked a great deal went through his entire life so petrified that he had to make up its substance at nearly every turn, a substance others clearly valued. Stephen was definitely this way. He did not like new opportunities. He hated meeting new people. He liked only old movies that he had already seen. And never would he backtrack through the roads of life, just in case, I imagine, there was something scary that was missed the first time that would have to be redefined away on a return visit.

I remember one dramatic demonstration of this very early in our relationship. We were on our way to a party put together by some soon-to-be friends. Stephen had spoken much about that coming evening, expressing concern for reasons that I did not and do not know. When it got close to departure time, he was fretting as always about his clothing, what his hair looked like. I finally got him out of the house a few minutes past the time we were supposed to be there. He insisted on driving so that he could have easier access to the mirrors to check and recheck the vital appearances. Neither of us was sure of the directions and we began to get on each other's nerves, debating the issues and questioning each other's motives in rather usual ways. As we approached the general neighborhood, we passed what should have been our turn because of bad street lighting. I pointed that out, and he smiled. He turned to me and said, with incredibly defining honesty and cruelty: "I'm sorry. I guess we missed that one."

"Just turn around," I said. "Here is a perfect place."

"Oh, no. I made my commitment a long time ago to always keep going forward." And forward we kept going that evening.

That incident frightened me more than I ever admitted, if for no other reason than it made me wonder just how long we could really expect to go anywhere in life without turning around to check our path, an idea never meant to be taken so literally. But I think that I also took it as a challenge to break him of that absurd belief and to assure him that sometimes it was all right to go backwards in the name of or in search of progress.

The physicalization and verbalization of death played a dramatic part in changing Stephen's need for and style of manipulation. So much so that he began to pick up my obsession with outright demonstrative honesty.

He began in the last few months to badger me fairly constantly about crying in front of his family. I never succeeded in giving him this victory, as I had found other outlets by then. I knew that he took this failure as a personal affront and with an enormous sense of frustration. But what he never knew was that part of the reason for my lack of change came from the fact that the sustainability of our love by that time was cemented in the existence of some of these games. They presented a challenge, an intrigue that distracted me from the daily rituals. Money problems, job problems, care-giving, a lack of confidence in the purpose and direction of life: each of these was becoming unbearable for me, and his need to try to survive could not focus on these concerns at all. So our cement began to disintegrate. So much so that when I would create straw persons about "What would life be like if . . . ?" during these down moments I honestly could not say that I wanted to continue living together. His manipulations and distortions defined excitement, and I did not want to give them up, even to the point of helping him on his journey to eternity.

"What did the snail say when he got on the back of the turtle? Wheeeeeee!"

That was one of the first jokes I remember Stephen telling some friends we met on one of the silly evenings we spent drinking wine and laughing, after we finally got to the point of being able to turn the car around when it was needed. At that time it was particularly funny, context being everything. But to me, it was so much more than that. I remember it as being the time when Stephen knew that we would be together for as long as possible. He was trying to demonstrate that he could convert his appreciation of my humor into something for himself. He was, if you will, practicing telling a joke. And learning to use the power of interaction to make friends and influence people. He never admitted it directly, but I suspect that there was much in what I had accomplished in life that he would have wanted to copy.

From the evening that we met we laughed a lot. Too much probably, although most of it was private. This set the tone of our relationship. We were not really seeing his family or other friends very much at that time, so we could spend more time wrapped up with each other's personalities. I wasn't making much money, and he had not yet started his future as a concierge. It was during this time that we could afford to laugh the most, and it was near the end of this time that he made his snail joke.

Unfortunately, this confidence was also setting him up for a second ultimate life fall as he failed to appreciate the troubles that can arise from having personal power, especially on the job. This time it would lead to his losing his job at the St. Francis Hotel.

He told me a story once about being at work on the day of an evening when the president of the United States (George Bush) was coming to the hotel for a speech. Secret Service agents were buzzing about. For the most part he ignored them, except to give them directions to nice places to eat and visit. There were several agents he had gotten to know pretty well and he felt comfortable joking with them. (They eventually gave him a plaque for "contributing to law enforcement" efforts. Seriously!)

On one occasion, the officers were apparently proud about how tight their security was. Stephen playfully insisted to them that it was not, and that he could get near the president without any problems. They disagreed. He told me later that he was going to wait and make his demonstration when the TV cameras were pointing at the president, but he decided instead to be nice to his policing buddies and not to risk an arrest. So he had one of them paged to the staging area. At the same time, when no one was expecting it, he popped out, on stage, next to where the president would eventually be, using a hidden hallway door created during Prohibition. He was carrying a sign that said "Gotcha!"

The Secret Service agents thought it funny, knowing that Stephen was just joking. Stephen's management was less impressed, perhaps from fear of bad publicity. The agents came to Stephen's rescue to make sure that he would not get in trouble. But it was perhaps the first of the nails in his professional coffin. He later learned that having power through verbal skills can be dangerous and threatening. In fact, he ultimately lost his job because of managers who feared for the way he very skillfully found his way about for the benefit of his clients.

I can still see how this experience in and of itself could have shaken his faith in humor and fantasy, because he truly resented the loss of his career. But it did not, even with the blow of the diagnosis, sad though he often became thinking about his work.

So he filled his time redefining life. Stephen was sort of growing a new habit of getting mad at people from time to time whenever he thought they were not living up to his expectations (which included not giving him the attention or goodies he felt due). He did this quite often with his sisters, as I saw it, and to a lesser extent with his parents and me. His favorite way was to identify some issue that bothered him, dramatize it after some mundane incident, and continue harping on it until something happened that confirmed that Stephen was right all along. Then, with the issue settled in his mind, he would stop talking to that person with an infamous silent treatment until he or she would acknowledge that he was correct. Only when Stephen thought it was time to give up the lesson would the circumstances change, and all would be right again.

This was definitely a family game, founded in some unknown characteristic of the clan. But it was very serious to Stephen. And he did not count it as being funny when it was happening. But the way he used it changed with the maturity of his sense of humor. So dramatic was this transformation that, approaching the end of one of these episodes, he began to joke with me as we lay in bed. He made fun of himself for doing it and retraced the silly things he had done to a sister he deeply cared for. He tried to convince us both that no one had taken him seriously, of course, with hurt in his eyes and heart. I admit that I was already tuned out because this game had frustrated me more than anything else in our relationship; but there is no doubt that what he was doing was turning his deepest insecurities into a joke—a joke of which he and his actions were the butt.

I will never forget the most touching of these little life reversals. It was the day after his doctor had basically told him that there was nothing more medicine could do for him: he was going to die, and soon. He was lying in his bed at Alta Bates Hospital in Berkeley,

California. I walked in from breakfast at the cafeteria. His doctor had just arrived as well, checking on how he was. She was sitting near him looking at his file and telling him some inane point about yet another hopeless treatment they could try if he wanted to. As I approached, he looked up and said, "Hi. I'm glad you're back. Claire was just telling me that, you know, all the bad news she told me yesterday? Well, she was wrong; she had been reading someone else's file."

The look of astonishment on the doctor's face—and probably mine as well—demonstrated just how much we had been caught off-guard. We were both feeling so terrible that we did not know what to do.

Stephen did, smiling to us both in one of the biggest grins of his life. He had affirmed our love and the laughter we had shared together. I know this because after the doctor left he said to me something that I didn't understand until much later, when I sat down to put some order and closure in place. He said: "That joke was all my you."

I thought it was the morphine talking. And maybe it was. I'm still not sure. I don't really even know if what we experienced through all our episodes was what the growing of a long-term relationship is supposed to be like. But who can really know what to expect of a long life on a short road? Then again, anticipating that we could ever really know what a mature relationship is all about might just be someone's idea of a joke that is never meant to be understood. Some day, Stephen, maybe you and I will understand. Thanks for trying.

I hope you don't mind if I share.

Toby Johnson and

Kip Dollar

-s e v e n-

c y c l e s   i n   t i m e

T O B Y   J O H N S O N

Kip and I first met when I went to the bank to open a checking account. He was the new accounts officer with a name, he joked, that sounded like the perfect nom de plume for a banker: Mr. Dollar. He was an attractive young man, a tall, rangy redhead—a look I've always thought of as one of my "types."

In fact, a few months earlier I'd ended a relationship with a young redhead, a medical student who'd moved on to do a residency on the East Coast. It was a natural break-up, but a very emotional one. I cried for days. When the mourning was over, I discovered I was much more in touch with feelings than I'd ever been. I was in my late thirties; according to the Jungian model of personality (which was the system I'd been drawn to in my training as a psychotherapist), age thirty-five is the start of "the second half of life" and, often, a time of personality transformation in which patterns sometimes reverse: thinking types (like me) become feeling types; introverts become extroverts.

Well, that may be overcomplicating things, but it explains why I turned bold that day at the bank, and as I got up to leave Kip's desk, I said, "You're a very nice-looking man. You remind me of my ex-boyfriend."

As Kip tells the story, those words echoed through the marble halls of that solemn old bank. He froze—perhaps having been "outed" more than he was ready for at work—but did manage a polite "thank you." In fact, he wasn't particularly outed by that occasion. But when, a couple of weeks later, I sent him a thank-you note, the whole department took notice. That was because I had something of a reputation. I'd moved back to my hometown, San Antonio, a couple of years before—from San Francisco, where I'd been trained as an out-front gay therapist and, through working with gay scholar Toby Marotta, had become a sort of authority on gay community organizing. By the time I came to the bank to open that account, I was "the gay therapist" in San Antonio, the chair of the San Antonio Gay Alliance, and a frequent spokesperson for the gay community on local TV.

Although Kip was not out at work at the time, he knew who I was, but certainly didn't let on to his co-workers. One of his supervisors, however, called him aside after my thank-you note arrived to "warn" him that "Toby Johnson is head of the homosexuals."

Over a period of a year I occasionally stopped by Kip's desk to say hello when I was at the bank. And when I called on business, he was the person I asked for because I knew he'd recognize my voice. At the end of a phone conversation one day, he suggested we get together for dinner.

That was the start of our relationship. We dated a couple of times before having sex. We moved in together after five months. About that time, Kip quit the bank and took a job in my family's company, a wholesale florist and trucking company for southern Texas. By becoming part of the family business, Kip became part of the family.

I had long before decided that at age forty-two I would retire from social services. At my twenty-eighth birthday, I'd had a sort of grand Jungian vision of my life fitting into five fourteen-year phases. I was just starting my career in mental health services then. That was going to be the opening of the third phase.

As time for its closure approached fourteen years later, Kip and I, then in our fourth year together, began to develop plans to move to the West Coast, buy a house out in the country, and open a small gay bed-and-breakfast. We did spend a summer in a beach town south of Santa Cruz—one of the nicest times of our lives—but did not find the property we wanted or the business opportunity. And, in fact, at the end of that summer, my mother's failing health brought us back to Texas. Coincidentally, a friend of ours who had opened a gay and lesbian bookstore in Austin, just up the highway from San Antonio, asked if we'd be interested in buying the bookstore from him. I'd just had my first gay novel published. Kip and I were looking to start a business together. This seemed like just the opportunity we were hoping for.

For seven years, we operated Liberty Books. As a former banker, Kip was great with numbers and money. As a "cultural activist," I was good at keeping up with what was in print. As a couple, we made an excellent management team for the store. It gave us a chance to prove to ourselves (and to our parents) that we could be successful in the way of American society.

It was a marvelous job. Central to communication in the gay and lesbian community, Liberty Books provided us a social and political role in Austin. We helped set a certain tone: we had a policy, for instance, that the store be a place one could feel comfortable bringing one's mother. We wanted to be very revolutionary, while also being very respectable. The bookstore was a wonderful way to contribute to the community. We performed in a gay guerrilla theater troupe. We attended all the community events. We quickly became recognized as a couple. And the social recognition by the community, in turn, contributed to the stability of our relationship. When we were asked to take part in a Valentine's Day demonstration for gay relationship rights, we agreed to be one of the forty-some couples who were going to apply for marriage licenses in a highly publicized zap. By the time the zap happened, however, it had gotten down to two couples: two lesbians and us. And briefly we made the national news.

For all our openness, Kip had never come out to two members of his immediate family, acquiescing to his mother's belief that these two men couldn't handle the information. As it turned out, both of these relatives were on a fishing trip together the weekend we hit the news, and both of them saw the story. To everybody's surprise they were quite supportive—even called to congratulate us on making headlines. (One of them turned out to have had a certain sort of gay history of his own!) Thus we became "poster boys" for gay marriage rights in Texas for a while and were the first gay male couple to register as domestic partners a few years later when Travis County (briefly) recognized such relationships.

By the mid-1990s, Austin was being called "silicon prairie" because of the influx of high-tech companies. A gay bookstore (and hip, sexy, porn movie rental) chain from Houston moved into town. A book "superstore" was opening a few blocks from our humble little independent store. Our old-fashioned business was going out-of-date. We sold the store to a gay bookstore chain from Dallas (which closed it for good eighteen months later).

While being Ozzie and Harriet for Austin's gay community, as we sometimes joked (especially when we were frustrated we weren't getting the kind of sexual attention that gay men are apt to want coming their way), we remodeled an old house in a gentrifying downtown neighborhood, lived with several housemates, built a friendship circle around us, and created for ourselves an identity as a successful and happy gay couple—and as good role models.

By 1997, our bonds to Texas having loosened after my mother's death, we turned our attention back to the dream of the country B&B. In a series of coincidences and strokes of luck, we found a marvelous place in the foothills of the Rocky Mountains outside Denver that's surprisingly like a fictional utopian colony in one of my novels. So now we're running the House of Peregrine's Perspective in Conifer, Colorado. We've adopted a whole new lifestyle now, living by ourselves, almost as hermits (at least until the B&B business gets going). It's a new phase of togetherness and commitment, just in time to usher in a new fourteen-year cycle.

For in 1998, Kip and I reached a milestone in our lives together. We have a difference in age between us of fourteen years. Our 1998 anniversary celebrated fourteen years together, with Kip at the age I was when we met.

Metaphorically—astrologically, mythologically, numerologically—fourteen is a significant number: a "Saturn return": double the mystical number seven. That Kip and I are fourteen years apart seems just perfect. In fact, the age difference, we both believe, has helped strengthen the relationship over the years. As Drew Mattison and David McWhirter, authors of *The Male Couple*, themselves about fourteen years apart, pointed out, a phase difference between members of a couple guarantees that they will be working on different life-stage issues and can support one another through these rather than reinforcing and amplifying the problems and anxieties of each stage.

In some ways, longevity is no issue at all. Indeed, it's inevitable with the passage of time. In other ways, of course, it's an achievement gained through decision, effort, and strength of character.

Kip and I identify three dynamics, which can be expressed in aphorisms, that have helped strengthen our relationship: "Love is a decision, not just an emotion"; "You're never upset for the reason you think"; and "Intend for the other what you want for yourself."

There have certainly been practical helps, like our good fortune in being able to own a business together and in having families that honored our relationship. But the big issues have always been the interpersonal and intrapersonal emotional states that make up the relationship. And these are addressed by the aphorisms.

"LOVE IS A DECISION, NOT JUST AN EMOTION."

In the first months of our relationship, I did the *est* Six-Day Course and Kip did the *est* Training. It gave us a common vocabulary for personal issues. These worked like Dumbo-feathers to create "safe space" in which we could talk through stuff. "I don't mean to make you wrong *and* I need to share . . ." has always been an initiation for a serious talk. The technique of using "and" instead of "but" has prevented so many disagreements from ever getting started.

An important piece of wisdom from *est* was that one can have a relationship with any-body. The magic isn't in the other person, it's in the willingness to communicate and work through problems and to take responsibility for one's own emotions. It was actually Erich Fromm's *Art of Loving* that made the point that love is a decision not an emotion.

Sexual attraction and some amount of psychological harmony are important, too. And that's why, to use an awful cliché, you have to kiss a lot of toads to find a prince. Human beings have "types" we're attracted to, and we have to honor this unconscious drive. It is what gets "limerence," infatuation, started in the first place. But inevitably limerence fades and decision takes over.

Kip and I started with a certain amount of limerence, although it was cultivated over months of seeing one another at the bank, then a couple of dates before jumping into sex. In the beginning, neither of us was exactly the other's idea of Mr. Right. We didn't start with "love at first sight," and I think we're luckier for it. We had the opportunity to decide we liked each other and would make good partners—not that I think we had any idea then that that was going to mean fourteen years ... and, apparently, the rest of our lives! But we did this deliberately because we found in each other a person we could trust, who valued relationship and had qualities we each honored.

Kip and I have made a decision to keep a certain amount of limerence alive by deliberately expressing affection frequently, giving each other a parting kiss every time one of us leaves the house, never going to bed angry, and always saying "I love you" as the last words of the day. These have been rituals that support the decision.

"YOU'RE NEVER UPSET FOR THE REASON YOU THINK."

Here's a notion from *A Course in Miracles*. It's also the basis of crisis intervention therapy and the theory of suffering and causation behind Buddhism. Kip and I joke that when one or the other of us gets stressed out, who else is there to blame but the other? And the ability to step outside the upset of the moment and see it's really not the other's fault is a saving grace. After all, the upset is really the recurrence of a pattern learned in childhood, old memories (what Werner Erhard called "a stack attack"), a rough day at work, a bad experience at the gym, and so forth. And we can allow ourselves the exercise of taking it out on each other, knowing that then, with insight, we can both let it go.

"INTEND FOR THE OTHER WHAT YOU WANT FOR YOURSELF."

Mahayana Buddhism expresses this idea in the notion that one of the proper abodes of the heart is "joy in the joy of others." This is also, of course, the basis of Jesus' Golden Rule, although in practice Christianity has tended to teach people to resent and disapprove of others' joy and (especially sexual) happiness. And, if there was a message we should have all learned from the so-called sexual revolution, it is this.

Because Kip and I have such an age difference between us, and because I'd lived in San Francisco through the party days of the 1970s, it was always important to me that I wish for Kip the breadth of (sexual) experience I'd been granted. He, after all, only got to the "party" as it was being closed down, and settling into marital bliss at twenty-five certainly promised to curtail his experience. I value the experiences that I had in San Francisco—although frankly I thought the party was terribly overrated. It's been important for me, and for both of us, that we balance our stock of experience. Primarily that's meant being liberal about sexual rules (although not about hygiene rules) and, especially, pursuing ways to share sexual adventures with other men together. "Monogamy," after all, means "one relationship," not poverty of experience.

Sometimes this has been easy; sometimes it's been difficult. What is important is the attitude of wanting for each other what we'd want for ourselves. We've expressed this in what we call the Brad Pitt Rule: "If Brad Pitt invites you to bed, you have permission to take him up on the offer—'cause if he invited me, I'd certainly want that." Too often lovers define their commitment around what they can't do, rather than what they will do for each other. That seems based in a heterosexist, patriarchal double standard in which men control women's behavior for the sake of certainty over their offsprings' genetic makeup. That model doesn't make any sense for gay men (and it's not helping straight people stay together).

Some of our most delightful adventures have been in group settings, like San Francisco's 1808 Club. Kip has a marvelous talent for gathering a group of admirers around him, and instead of niggardly choosing the most attractive for himself and running the others off, he gets everybody in the circle involved, so that nobody gets left out. That's the virtue we both strive to practice with each other and with other people: seeing to it that nobody feels left out.

After fourteen years, our sex isn't hot and hungry every night. Most of the time we pleasure ourselves and each other with the new high-tech marital aid of the VCR, a nice way to share together vicarious adventures with skin flick stars neither of us would have any chance of meeting otherwise and to make sure we're regularly experiencing the state of sexual arousal with each other. For in that altered state of consciousness, I think, we both connect with something deeply primal and transpersonal in human consciousness and merge our individual spirit and karmic selves with each other's in the very personal, intimate bonding of coming to orgasm together.

There's a fourth aphorism—that moves everything up to a mystical level—that is nicely expressed in a line from *Les Mis*: "Remember the words that once were spoken: to love another person is to see the face of God." I don't know where those words were supposed to have been spoken. This is not a notion that's part of orthodox religion. But it is a spiritual discovery of the new age of which gay liberation is also a part. "God" is not another thing in a universe of things. "God" is not a big person in the sky watching over us and having opinions. "God" is an aspect of, a metaphor for, our deepest selves, united with all other human beings who make up the planetary mind. "God" is the vitality of the planet that "wills" that all beings love life and enjoy experience. Since that experience manifests itself as flesh, that "God" really is the face of one's beloved. "God" is my best experience of being alive. And Kip and I have made a wonderful life by being that experience for one another: fourteen years of being "God" to the other's "God."

William Schmidt

and John Patton

- eight -

two travelers sharing a life

JOHN PATTON

Whenever people discuss the important actions that go into creating a long-term relationship, I usually stress that I think people should spend considerable time together before committing themselves to what they hope will be a permanent relationship. But then I think of the beginning of my relationship with Bill and I have to admit that it began in direct contradiction to this concept.

My relationship with Bill started in mid-August 1952, when I was living in San Francisco. I had come to California first thanks to the army, which had stationed me at Fort Ord. I was impressed with both the climate and the beauty of northern California, but at that time I had no idea that San Francisco had a special attraction for homosexuals. When I was about to graduate from college, I applied to several West Coast universities for graduate work, with the University of California at Berkeley as my first choice. I spent two years at UC-Berkeley, and after graduating with an M.A. in history and a B.L.S. in librarianship, I went to work in a library in San Francisco. At about this time I began going out to the bars almost every weekend. After a year of this, I was very weary of one-night stands.

One evening I went out to my favorite bar, where I met Bill, an attractive twenty-one-year-old who had driven to California with some friends at the end of his junior year at the University of Iowa. After we spent the weekend together, Bill moved into my small apartment to stay for the rest of his visit to San Francisco. By chance, my vacation was about to begin and I had planned to spend it going to Pennsylvania, where my family lived. So Bill and I decided that we would go back to Iowa together, and then I would continue on to Pennsylvania by myself. Neither of us had much money at that time, Bill because he was a student and I because I had only been working for a year, so we decided that we could only afford to go back to the Midwest on the bus.

Our trip to Iowa took several days because we stopped in Cheyenne so that we could get a good night's sleep. We still have snapshots taken during our stopover in Cheyenne. Traveling by bus is not the most comfortable way to travel and that was particularly the case back in the fifties, when most of the roads were only two lanes wide and went through all the small towns along the way. On the bus you got weary of sitting, and the food was pretty awful at the bus stops in those days. I stress the unpleasant aspects of the trip because I have always felt that these conditions had much to do with how our relationship developed. We both got along very well on the trip, and I think that spending several days together in a less than perfect situation gave us an excellent idea of how well we could cope. When we reached our destination in Iowa City, where Bill had an apartment, I recall our being very much in love, and I cannot remember any problems that occurred between us.

After spending a few days with Bill in Iowa City, I went to Pennsylvania to visit my family. I then returned to California with a short stopover in Iowa City to spend what might have been my last days with Bill. I still remember Bill with tears in his eyes as I said good-bye before boarding the bus for California. For both of us, this was the first love affair that we had ever had.

During the next few weeks, Bill and I exchanged letters and phone calls. However, I could not see what our future was going to be because we were separated by hundreds of miles and Bill would not be coming to California again until he graduated in the following spring. I wondered if it was possible to keep up a relationship for that length of time. So after much debate, I decided to resign from my job in California and go to Iowa to be with Bill until he finished college.

In order to get back to Iowa, I needed a job there. After a short correspondence with the library at the University of Iowa, I was offered a temporary job for six months, which, although the salary was low, would be sufficient. So I resigned from my library position in San Francisco in November and traveled by train to Iowa City toward the end of December. As it happened, by the time I made my reservations, it worked out that I arrived in Iowa City on Christmas Eve. Thus the anniversary of Bill's and my living together dates from Christmas Eve 1952.

After spending Christmas and a few days after it in Iowa City, Bill and I took Bill's old Chevy and drove to Fort Madison in southern Iowa to spend a few days with his family, which consisted of his parents and his twelve-year-old brother. Over the years, we were to see his parents many times and his brother later in California.

For the first eight months of 1953, Bill and I lived in a small apartment in Iowa City, where we established a routine of my working at the library and Bill's attending classes and of our socializing on weekends with members of the surprisingly active gay community in Iowa City. We found that neither of us particularly liked to cook, but we generally ate our meals at home. We both shared in household activities, such as cooking and cleaning the apartment, and on weekends we went to the grocery store together to do our shopping.

Although my temporary library position had originally been for six months, it was extended for an additional two, which meant that we could stay in Iowa City through August. We were glad for the additional money that I could save by working through the summer, and after school ended Bill found a job as an aide working in a psychiatric hospital in Cedar Rapids. Unfortunately, the job was for the afternoon shift, so Bill and I did not see much of each other during the week that summer.

From the beginning we planned to return to California after Bill graduated, so as the summer drew to its end we began to plan the trip. I decided first to go east to visit my family, while Bill went to southern Iowa to see his family. Because we thought that we would like to see Mexico, we decided to return to California that way. Since I had relatives in San Antonio, Texas, Bill and I thought we might meet there to begin our trip back to California together. It happened that my unmarried aunt, who lived in Texas, was driving back from New England to Texas in September, so I arranged to travel from Pennsylvania to Texas with her and her longtime friend. (These two women lived together for over thirty years, yet my aunt never hinted that she understood my relationship with Bill and, much to my annoyance, even was urging me to marry when I was in my forties!) We also planned that Bill would meet us in Memphis at the Greyhound Bus Depot at a certain day and time. Our plans for meeting worked out without a hitch, and after picking Bill up in Memphis, we drove on to Arkansas to spend the night at a motel. I still remember the great happiness it was for Bill and me to be together again.

After spending a few days with relatives in Texas, Bill and I took the bus to Mexico City. We spent several weeks in Mexico, visiting the tourist sites and traveling to Taxco and Cuernavaca. I like to ride on trains, so I convinced Bill to go along on a trip on a narrow-gauge railroad from Cuautla to Puebla, an all-day trip which included cold in the morning, heat in midday, and a thunderstorm and then cold and mosquitoes at night. This trip was probably the beginning of Bill's dislike of train travel.

From Mexico City we headed back to the United States by bus via the West Coast. When we got to Mazatlan, we found that the comfortable buses we had been on disappeared and we had to ride on old buses, the reason being that the road north had not been paved yet and the bus lines did not want their better buses used on the route. So it was a fairly uncomfortable trip north, twice involving our crossing rivers on a raft while the bus forded the river. Finally, we crossed the border at Nogales, and it was a great relief that we found a clean motel and a restaurant serving food we were used to. From Arizona we traveled by bus to San Francisco, arriving there in November.

Our most important task after returning to San Francisco was to find jobs. Looking back on that time, I am still amazed at how little money we had. As I recall, I had somewhere between two and three hundred dollars, and Bill, I seem to recall, had about sixty left. Even though the cost of living was, of course, much lower then, it still seems very little for two people to live on, neither of whom had work.

I did not find any library positions open in the area at first, which was very discouraging. However, just by chance, when checking with the California Civil Service employment office, the clerk happened to mention that there was a position open at Agnews State Hospital outside San Jose, a job which required two years of experience. Fortunately, I had just completed two years of library work, so I went to Agnews to see about the job. It turned out that the position had been open for nearly a year, so I was hired almost at once.

Within a few days Bill and I went to San Jose, found a small apartment, and celebrated Thanksgiving 1953 by settling in San Jose. A short time later, Bill applied for and got a position at Agnews as a psychiatric technician.

For the next two years we lived in San Jose. While I continued working at Agnews, Bill quit his job in September 1954 to attend San Jose State, where he took courses to obtain his teaching credentials. Although we did not know anyone when we moved to San Jose, we soon met a few people. At that time there were several gay bars in San Jose and one in particular we liked. So we dropped into the bar occasionally on weekends. Also, I met people at the hospital and we went to parties at their place, played cards at our place, or visited some of the people we had met at the bar.

The final phase in our moving from place to place occurred in August 1955, when we bought a small tract house in southern Alameda County. Although I remember thinking that we would probably move on in four or five years, we have lived in the same house ever since. Bill had received his teaching credentials and obtained a position teaching art in a high school in the Hayward District, where he stayed until he retired at fifty-five. And over the following years I held several library positions in the area until I retired at the age of sixty.

When Bill and I started living together, although we had had college roommates, this was the first time either of us had been in what we regarded as a permanent relationship. This meant we had to work out how we would handle situations in which we disagreed on what we wanted to do. We differed in our family backgrounds: I had had a close younger brother, but Bill essentially grew up as an only child because his brother was nine years younger. It thus developed that Bill handled situations by giving in or not discussing them because he had had no experience with dealing with the back-and-forth arguments of siblings, whereas I found it normal to argue. As time has passed, our method of handling situations has been to undertake little discussion and either quickly reach an agreement or else postpone action, if possible. When the situation only affects one of us, he usually goes ahead and does it and the other accepts it.

In the area of sexual relations, we have had no big controversy, unlike many couples. After a year or two, we accepted the fact that our relationship was not a monogamous one, although neither of us was particularly active in pursuing other lovers. We had no violent arguments about this, nor, in fact, have we had screaming fights or physical violence about any controversy.

When we started living together, we never thought about how we would assign tasks to ourselves. Unlike heterosexual marriages in which society has assigned certain areas of responsibility to each sex, there were no such assumed roles for us except that both being males, we expected to find certain tasks that neither wanted to do. That was not the case, however, and in the beginning we shared most duties. Since we were living in a rental unit, we had few housekeeping duties other than cooking and a small amount of cleaning. As I have said, neither of us likes to cook, but from the first we ate most of our meals at home, as we have continued to do. Although for years we went grocery shopping together, it finally dawned on us that it makes more sense to go separately rather than both of us spending time doing it. Also, over the years, we fell in the habit of each of us generally doing certain tasks in the kitchen; thus Bill usually does the entree while I do the salad and vegetable. Bill makes the rice and noodles, I do the mashed potatoes. We have always shared in the cleaning of the house, although I am more likely to do the sweeping and Bill the dusting.

Because I enjoy keeping busy, I tend to do most of the general maintenance jobs such as painting, both inside and out, keeping up the fences, and making other repairs to the house. Originally we both worked in building fences and laying out the yard with walks, patios, flower beds, and so forth. However, over the years, I have ended up doing most of the yard work because I like it more than Bill does.

The one area where we have had difficulty has been in furnishing the house, because we often do not agree on what we like. So if we need a new chair, for example, it may go for months or years before we buy one. And since we have ended up with compromises, the house is not furnished the way either of us would do it were he living alone. This is one area where heterosexual marriages may have the advantage since the wife often makes most of the decisions in equipping the house so it ends up pretty much being what she wants. In our case, neither of us was willing to let the other take over this responsibility alone.

Except when Bill was going to school, we have always kept separate financial accounts and shared only the expenses in maintaining the house. We have bought and maintained our own cars, have our own TV sets and our own furniture in our bedrooms. We both have liked this arrangement since it gives us the ability in some areas to express our own interests. We put the sales slips or bills for any expenses relating to the house in a small tin box and settle up the accounts at the end of each month. What we do with any money we have left over has always been up to each of us to spend or invest as he wishes.

One of the advantages of working in the education field is the fact that we had about ten weeks off in the summer. That meant that when I started working in 1958 as a librarian in a school (later in a community college), we could travel. Over the years we have made several trips by car around the western United States, traveling especially to see the architecture of Frank Lloyd Wright, Bill's great interest. We even managed to catch a glimpse of Wright in 1958 when we were visiting his studio at Taliesin West. In 1961 we had some friends stay in our house while we went to Europe for ten weeks for the "grand tour," which included most of western Europe from Spain and Italy to Scandinavia. Then in 1965 we applied for sabbaticals for 1965-66 at our respective school districts. Bill received his, but my district vacillated so long on making up its mind that I resigned and went anyway. During that trip of ten months, we covered much of Europe again, including a couple of months on the Riviera in late fall, and also went to Egypt, Lebanon, and Turkey. We bought a car in Denmark and drove to the Riviera, but left it there while we made our trip to the Middle East. We returned to the Riviera in March, drove the car to Amsterdam, and shipped it to New York. We drove our VW back to California, with stops at my parents' home in Pennsylvania, with Bill's parents in Iowa, and with my relatives in Texas. In the next few years we returned to Europe three times, the last time being in 1976.

Our social life has generally been fairly conservative. Since we live in the suburbs, we have had fewer opportunities to meet people. We found that when we met people in San Francisco or in Marin and Contra Costa Counties, we eventually lost contact because the drive there discouraged keeping up the relationship. Most of our friends we have met through work; the only long-time friend we met in a bar was each other. In earlier years we had a mix of heterosexual and gay friends, but in more recent years most of our friends have been gay. For several years we had a bridge club in which the four of us took turns entertaining. Recently we have lost several of our friends due to various diseases of aging, so that our socializing has become fairly limited.

There are times when we wonder about the future, what we will do should one of us have a long-term illness or when one of us dies. However, there is no way of dealing with that now.

If we have to, we will go to a retirement home. For the time being, we plan to continue living in our present house, where I will maintain the yard as long as I can, and eventually may hire a gardener. Since we retired, we both have been very content with our life. We both like to read, which fills many hours of our day. Bill works with his collection of books and such about Frank Lloyd Wright and other architects. He also started a postcard collection of architectural cards and now has several thousand of them, which he arranges, looks at, and consults, and he also goes to an occasional show to buy more. I keep busy with yard work and maintenance work, reading, walking—I usually walk three or four miles several times a week—and in 1995 I bought a computer with which I spend a small amount of time. We usually take one day a week on our own to go to San Francisco or Berkeley or Oakland for shopping or movies or whatever. We also go to movies and eat out occasionally near our home. Several times a month we entertain or visit friends. Bill watches more TV than I do, but neither of us tends to watch it until after dinner. So for now, I think we can both say that the years since we retired have been the happiest ones of our life.

Davidson Lloyd

and Tom Keegan

-nine-

i'll love you forever

DAVIDSON LLOYD

In the summer of 1977 the beverage industry forever changed our drinking habits. They unveiled the stay-put-opener-tab. No longer could we fling those metal openers into the wilds, to clog the beaks of seagulls and throats of dolphins. That metal tab "stayed put." That aluminum trigger became a symbol of my own longevity.

That same summer my sexual desires took a similar change, from women to men. *Man!* Tom Keegan had red hair and blue eyes, and his nearness caused nervousness in my stomach, confusion in my psyche, and constant hardness below my belly. I was having orgasms of the heart over a *man!* Maybe it was the sun, the beach, the sand, the scent of beach plums, the scent of suntan lotion, the diesel scent of arriving and departing island ferries. Maybe I was caught up in the trance of a summer-stock romance, a condition often suffered when you're on an island. An island fever that burns your skin, your reason, and your heart.

Maybe it was the scent of his hair, a touch of sea water, a touch of honeysuckle shampoo. Maybe it was the scent of his breath, that cavity that engulfed my tongue with sweet sloppy wetness. Maybe it was the scent of his body, sweating from rehearsing, swimming, a body scent that smelled of outdoor activities, not apartment hibernation.

Maybe it was the scent that lingered in the red hairs that crowned his genitals. Maybe it was the scents of our lovemaking that thinly coated our bodies: oils, creams, sweat, cum, as we lay in each other's arms, drifting in and out of dozing, not realizing what we were getting into. Lazing in the dying light of late afternoon, smoothing aloe vera on his translucent, freckled skin, sunburned red velvet, and feeding him ice cream to soothe his insides, I blurted out, "I've never felt this way about *anyone* before. I've never felt this way about a *man!*" He turned his face to me, seated on the edge of the bed.

"I don't tan, I just burn. It runs in my family. What *are* you feeling?" As softly as I applied the lotion, it still drew white spots where my fingers touched. Pain flushed his face. Tears came to my eyes. I didn't know why. Sometimes you just cry with no meaning attached.

"I think I'll love you forever," I whispered.

"I'll love you forever" became our private little joke, from the moment we fell, love at first sight, into each other's arms and bed, on Martha's Vineyard. We were in residence at a summer arts colony there. We had never met before. I was standing at the top of the stairs; he was standing at the bottom of the stairs, and "something happened," something passed between us and locked our hearts into a connection so strong, so ancient. A feeling so powerful, so intimate, a feeling that might be as rare as catching two identical snowflakes. Some call it twin flame, soul mate, dual spirits. It was too tender to have a name with us.

"I'll love you forever" seemed old-fashioned and too romantic for those times. We were very aware of the warm impermanence of same-sex relationships. After all, it was the "f---for all" and "all for f---ing" waning 1970s. Sex was in; romance was for novels. You weren't supposed to form a relationship, live with someone, relate to them, share a whole life together, buy sheets and underwear, walk down the aisle of a supermarket like a couple and not like roommates shopping for bologna and available boys. There was too much fun to be had; too much disco, too many highs, too many bodies, not enough lubricant.

I asked him to come live with me in New York. "I'll move in with you until I find my own apartment." He moved in and twenty years passed quicker than the minute waltz played in thirty seconds.

The seventies shifted abruptly into the 1980s. Reagan rode to power, bearing Nancy on his shoulders, and suddenly there was Trouble in River City. If gays and lesbians thought they were "in the room" but at the children's table, they soon discovered that there was "no place at any table." We were outside, stranded in the tsunami of AIDS that was burning our faces like winter along Michigan Avenue. A change faster than a yuppie could close escrow. We clung to one another and kept our vision of coupledom, with little support from hets and homos alike, struggling, stumbling, making it up as we went along, falling, but mostly flying.

Who can remember twenty years? A lot happened in twenty years. The world turned, and there were moments when we thought it might spin out of existence. There was the ERA, IRA, PLO, ET, BeeGees, CBs, and O.J. Jimmy, Ronnie, Georgie, and Billy all slept in the Lincoln Room, although not at the same time. Oscars went to *Amadeus, Annie, Rocky, Kramer, Gandhi,* and *Gump.*

We took each day one at a time, sometimes. We attended the marches, fretted when the wrong guy got into power, rejoiced when a simple victory occurred, although it came through struggle and pain. We traced the subtle indentations of lines in our faces, measured the forward march of age, watched the flow of information cram its way into our consciousness and fill us up with endless technology on how to experience the slicing of a potato without leaving the couch.

I have photographs, postcards, reviews, from our growing repertoire of theater works: *Fragile Bodies; Passing on the Right & Other Accidents of Life; Men, Matrimony & 9th Avenue Mystics; Naked & In Love;* and *The Last Queer Taboo.* We produced twenty theater pieces, three kids' shows, and two screenplays. I have scattered mementos of travel. A tiny bronze horse from Athens; a shell from the North Sea, which I placed against my stomach to remind me that my partner was collecting shells along the Mediterranean while I was performing at the Edinburgh Theater Festival in Scotland. We sifted, shifting back and forth, about what to call each other in those days: lover, friend, significant other, companion, soul mate, twin flame, spouse, sex buddy, roommate, trick, settling on "husband."

I have the detailed letters, the detailed daily events, as he went off on his own spiritual quest to India for ten weeks. One goes off; one waits. Like a child I laid out ten pairs of socks, removing one pair for each week that he was gone, until all that was left was a pair of nylon socks with a Christmas wreath design.

I remember fragments. Pieces of memory. All gone; all passed so quickly. I snatch a glimpse of our making love under a waterfall on the Big Island of Hawaii, among the hundreds of lovemaking images that inhabit my physical memory. A corner of quiet memory, sitting silently in our apartment in New York, watching the sun slither down the shaft of the Empire State Building. A piercing reminder of the financial struggles of being an openly out, performing couple.

A torn memory of our first fight. He hit me on my thigh. (I insulted him, he said.) We had spats, fights, arguments, silent nights of lying side by side and not speaking, but feeling the heat of wanting to touch, to break through the separation. The voice of the mind, not the heart, that whispers, "If I were alone . . ." Each time we struggled, through pain, hurt, past relationship baggage, family, childhood, the overstimulation and stress from living in the latter part of the twentieth century, plagued by a growing medical crisis and an economy that was ballooning to the point of depression thinness. When we couldn't work it out ourselves, we resorted to the first secret to long-term relationships. Therapy!

As our time together grew longer we met the challenges as they emerged: society, the government, hairstyles, past lives, family, friends, financial stability, paper versus plastic, intimacy, sex, disco, dishes, death, privacy, boundaries, being buffed, family values, roles, homo home ownership, stereotypes, internalized homophobia, getting too settled, settling for comfort. Then came *Marriage*. So we did. Ceremony, family, friends, commitments, recycled pawn shop wedding bands, a cake, vows, and like Lucy and Ricky drove across America to live in California. We were just getting settled in Los Angeles when Tom's best, Mark, died. He was part of our wedding, now we were part of his death.

There is nothing like the constant shadow of death to bring you up short, to remind you of your own mortality, to reassure you that you are not invincible from the sting of death's fatal suck. Sudden illness stops your breath; death brings the breadth of tears.

Friends were leaving. My first was Rob, who died of AIDS when AYDS was a weight-loss program. A wasting body, gray before his years, the scent of illness emanating beneath the sheets that his hand kept darting under to dab with French cologne. He lay in St. Vincent's Hospital, close to dementia. "When I get out of here, I'm going to buy a Maserati," he yelled to no one in particular. "How are you going to get those long legs of yours in a Maserati?" I chided back. I knew he would never draw his legs to the side of the bed; this was his last stop. My tears tumbled onto Seventh Avenue as I stumbled blindly home. Sometimes tears have meaning attached.

Hospital visits became frequent outings; memorials became current events. Left and right they marched out. Some with great fanfare; some going silently into that good night. No discrimination here. Generations were being rapidly decimated. One day healthy, the next reduced to old men before their time. Doctors, scientists, and social service professionals were predicting that every one would be infected or dead by the millennium. I prayed that they were wrong. I prayed that we would remain healthy—not just from AIDS, but from any illness.

I assumed we were safe. (What is safe?) Tom was my first male relationship, but there were some one-night stands before him. The experts were reporting a gestation period for AIDS-related symptoms up to ten years. Paranoia needs but little suggestion to spread. Could one of us be carrying death in our veins? We never bothered to use plastic, never bothered to draw a drape across our genitals, in our lovemaking, since neither one of us had been with anyone else since we met (or so we thought). Skin to skin felt too good. Why dress it up and diminish that sensation, that naked pleasure?

In those days you learned about the death of someone in offhanded ways. You might pass someone coming out of a subway train, as you're entering, and they would say, "Did you hear about so-and-so?" Of course, you knew what they meant. It wasn't like so-and-so had found a great job, or found a rent-controlled apartment, or found Mr. Right. No response was needed. You took the information into your day, into yourself, into your history.

The gay magazines printed obituaries on a weekly basis. Pictures! Bios! A endless gallery of death images. I looked at them with trepidation, not wanting to find a face there that would leap out at me. But I had to look. If I didn't find a familiar face there, among the primarily young photos, I felt physically, emotionally, and psychically reprieved. I never saw Kenny's photo, he came to me at Broadway and Seventy-second Street, on one of my annual visits back to the Big Apple.

I was crossing against the light, dodging oncoming cars, when I ran into Chris. I hadn't seen her in years. She is one of those women who never seem to age. We had been in a lavish street production of Benjamin Britten's *Noye's Fludde*. I played the Dove, leading hundreds of Manhattan school kids onto a flatbed truck that was the Ark. We performed in Times Square, when the homeless, alcoholics, and drug addicts called Forty-second Street "home." I had this outrageous headdress and makeup consisting of blue and silver sequins glued to my face. I looked like one of the last remaining drag queens parading the Great White Way. It was a perfect setting for the end of the world flood.

"Did you hear about Rob?" were the first words out of her mouth. Rob had played God from high in a cherry picker, wearing a fifty-foot cape, adorned with labels from cans, boxes, candy wrappers. God of merchandise. Yes, I had buried Rob. "Have you seen Kenny?" she said. I froze. (Kenny had also been in this production.) "He's gone too," she added. Chris had a way of listing deaths as if she were sorting drugs from vitamins and trying to remember which she had taken last.

A memory distracted me and I found myself becoming distant, disconnecting from her words. I had had a little "thing" with Kenny. It was in what I called my bisexual days. Kenny was truly a waif, almost otherworldly. Today he would fit perfectly into an alien scenario. He seemed trapped on this planet, in this century. He might have been living a past life in his present life. He had an androgynous quality, a *puer aeternus* quality. Boy energy, yet an aura of the female. Not transgender. A boy-girl. I found his androgyny completely seductive.

How we first connected I don't remember. Once in a while I would go with him to his apartment on the Upper West Side. He never wanted to come home with me. (I lived alone then.) Kenny liked to suck on me. I liked him to suck on me. He was a little animal at it, fiercely enjoying, while I got fiercely off. He never let me suck on him. I was a virgin when it came to male sex. "Virgins are so boring," he said. "They haven't the slightest idea about what to do."

"You could teach me," I suggested.

"Let someone else teach the virgins of the world, I like a man who knows what goes where and when." I let him have his way. I also topped him from time to time.

Once I got involved with Tom, I never saw Kenny again. Nonetheless, my own paranoia began to build on hearing of his death. The simplest thing could bring it on. A scratch that took three days to heal, rather than two; a winter cold that lingered a little too long; a loose bowel movement that could escalate into diarrhea.

My sexual history was limited, but Kenny was part of that experimentation. Kenny was PT (prior Tom). Tom and I had been together so long that I assumed we were both negative. (But no one really knew!) The whole "testing" and "telling" of one's status in the gay community was taboo. It fell into the category of "Don't ask, don't tell." Getting tested came up, but neither of us seemed overly anxious to know. Not knowing took a lot of energy.

Without telling him, I went to get tested. In the waiting room of the community clinic, a video was in progress. A huge, flesh-colored, rubber dildo filled the screen. A female voice, with airline stewardess intonations, instructed the viewer: "Once the penis is erect, roll the condom gently over the head of the penis, leaving a little bubble at the tip, recoiling it down to the base of the shaft." The diverse group: men, women, teenagers, all races, all creeds, some so clean-cut I wondered if they had ever touched a penis. Some with piercings and tattoos to rival a gypsy. It was required viewing before bloodletting. We all shared two qualities: nervousness and fear.

The bloodletting was quick and anonymous. A medical assistant with a plastic mask hiding his face, making him anonymous, tied a rubber cord around my upper arm. My virgin vein rose up like the swollen Mississippi River, and his needle poised above it to take a drink.

Now, being a coward to pain and blood, I warned the needle man. "I don't like the sight of blood," I tentatively ventured, not to appear too much of a sissy. "Don't be surprised if I faint."

"Don't be surprised if you lie there," the voice behind the mask quipped. He laughed; I laughed, and the needle dove into my arm and drank its fill.

The wait. Waiting is harder than making the leap to get tested. Waiting gives you endless space to worry, get depressed, make yourself sick, or convince yourself that you don't have AIDS and shouldn't have bothered with the test at all, or you've been fooling yourself and you are HIV+ and should probably put in a emergency call to Dr. Death. If I tested negative I would be relieved, but guilty. I wouldn't be part of "the club," and therefore considered not as good a gay man as its "positive" members. It was nuts, but you could feel the anger around positive or negative statuses. Damned if I was; damned if I wasn't. One was not better than the other. Most gay men kept silent about their status, and therefore avoided both camps.

Tom was not pleased when I revealed to him that I had gotten tested. I thought that I was being brave, forthright, proactive, but he didn't take it that way. He thought that we should have discussed it and then made a joint decision to get tested. It was as if I had betrayed our coupledom in some way. He didn't seem interested in my results; didn't seem interested in my secret non-status, which was no longer a secret. I knew! "I'm negative," I announced.

I read in *Cosmopolitan* magazine that it's not a bad thing to have a secret in a relationship. It gives you something to hold on to. It gives your partner something to yet find out about you. Tom had a secret. His secret brought the wolf to our door. A secret "little thing" with an older, secretly gay, married man, with a wife and four kids in the suburbs. One day, the son of the older man called to say that Murray, his father, was in the hospital with AIDS and that Tom had given it to him. He threatened Tom. Murray! Couldn't he be a Bruce, or Biff?

I lost my head, lost control. I blamed him for not telling me sooner! My negative status seemed jeopardized. I pulled away. I became sullen, and when he tried to get close, to get us to talk about it, like all the other issues that had challenged our years together, I shut down, shut the entrance to my heart and sealed it with hardness. (I learned this from my family.) I couldn't deal with the negative-positive possibilities. "You've killed us both!" I shouted. I demanded that he get tested.

He resisted, but finally agreed, going to the same bloodletting clinic as I did, to an anonymous surgical mask that confidentially drained blood from his virgin arm. Days passed. I attempted to go on with the ordinary events of my life, but hypochondriac neurotic that I am, that was impossible. Every inch of my body became a potential death field. I noticed that we seemed cool with each other during his waiting period. The Waiting Game gave me time for my own soul-searching.

We were house-sitting in Malibu when he got his results. Up a canyon, with mountains outside the balcony and the Pacific, blue, in the distance, the sun disappearing behind the hills far to the north. Another beautiful southern California sunset. All seemed right with the world, as day put itself to sleep; all seemed in harmony. Nature dealt with fires, floods, mud slides, howling winds, the earth cracking open. We could deal with positive-negative.

When he came in the door, we embraced. There are times when you embrace and it is just a hug, a friendly greeting, and there are times when both bodies merge into each other,

I'LL LOVE YOU FOREVER

98

energies mingle and swirl around inside both of you. We held on to each other for a long time, our strengths binding us, all our years together passing through our psyches and bringing us to this moment, the present. It was real; the feelings were real; his tears on my cheek were real; my stomach shaking with emotion was real; our friends' dog lapping at our legs was real.

"I don't want to know," I declared. "I was a fool! I love you! I promised to take care of you. When I get scared I can become an emotional assassin. I lash out, but my heart brings me back to you. I don't care about your results. One is not better than the other. They're both states of being. Conditions to be shared and cared for, no matter what they are. I was stupid to place one above the other. You are the only thing I place higher than anything." All this tumbling out of me in one breath.

He led me to the couch. We sat, silent for the longest time, occasionally touching, fingers feeling fingers, a hand to the side of the face, a hand stroking a shoulder, moving down to the muscle. We were solid and together. Negative-positive meant nothing. It could not define us, could not divide us. We had defined each other the moment our eyes met. Nothing could alter that power. He didn't need to share his blood report with me. I knew! I knew all along. I hadn't trusted my intuition.

I was remembering; remembering all we had shared together. My body trembled. I felt renewed, redeemed, closer to him, pledged again. I slid the palm of my hand into his. We spoke our wedding vows: "I promise to be here for you," I stated.

"I promise to be your partner," he replied. Tom came to his last vow, "I promise that wherever I am and whatever I'm doing I will remember that we are together."

Some time later, Tom received a hastily scribbled note from Murray, written on the back of a flyer for a children's show that Murray had done when he was much younger. He apologized for his son's behavior. He did not have AIDS; he had had a nervous breakdown worrying about AIDS. His secret was spilled, and he was doing damage control. "For the sake of my family," he wrote, "I don't think we should have any future contact, even as friends." Tom said he was sad that Murray needed to end their friendship. We were closing doors, behind which Murray and Kenny might find solace with one another. An older spirit and a younger ghost.

It is winter! We are in the first five years of living and working together. Outdoors the scent of snow descends gently down onto Third Avenue. Inside Performance Space 122 the aerosol scent of spray paint powders the air, sending a fine blue mist drifting down to the floor. The audience is deep, rows of men seated on chairs, overflowing onto the floor, body after body, the performing area diminished by all these male bodies, male energy, male scents.

Across a white backdrop carefully printed words appear: *"I'll love you forever . . ."* My hand moves across the paper, inscribing each letter clearly with the flair of a young lover tagging his affection on the side of a vacant building. Satisfied, I move down to sit with all those male bodies attending our performance.

Tom leaps to the screen. His reply, red aerosol letters, to match his flaming red hair, not careful, not printed, a flair for sloppiness, that answers the latter phrase, *". . . or at least until Friday!"* The audience bursts into laughter. It binds a pact, an agreement, a fragile commitment.

Now, after twenty years of living and working together; after touching his skin to my skin and feeling that shared electricity; after inhaling his every scent into my being; after countless hours of lovemaking, feeling him deep inside of me, or me in him; after lying with him in tears or anger or mutual silliness; after sharing hours of couple commonplaceness; after birthing and deathing family and friends; after unwrapping ourselves to each other (and there is always more to unfold), our "I'll love you forever . . . or at least until Friday" sentiment has proven to be our lasting commitment to one other.

And where are we now: we're on the same page, crossing the bridge to the twenty-first century, where the Web awaits and the millennium is calling, where "I'll love you forever . . . or at least until Friday" is our eternal Friday, and that Friday is beyond time and space, but part of our future.

Barry Losinsky

and George Matthews

-ten-

through it all

BARRY LOSINSKY

C ome on over. There are a couple of numbers I want you to check out," Fred whispered and then hung up the phone. Fred, my best friend, had also become my gay mentor and "mother." He enjoyed sharing his wealth of information and varied experiences in the gay world.

The back roads to Fred's had finally been plowed nearly clear of the sixteen inches of snow that had arrived with the new year. The moon glistened through the bare branches of trees and cast eerie reflections on the untouched drifts as I cautiously maneuvered down the quarter-of-a-mile drive on this chilly winter's evening. I recognized Fred's XKE, of course, but not the other car or the pickup parked under the flood-lit slippery elm in front of the old stone colonial home.

I was extremely apprehensive. I was 5'9", and I weighed 170 pounds. Although it had been six years since I had lost 100 pounds, and although my waist was ten inches smaller than it had been in my prime, my mind had yet to catch up to my untoned body. In my head I was still fat and just as undesirable as before.

At twenty-six I was still attempting to adjust to the sexual orientation that I had finally begun to accept as true. The task was particularly difficult in light of societal dictates and my Jewish religion, which made it clear that if I had these "unnatural" desires, then I must be sick. Or at the very least defective and contemptible. I wasn't quite a virgin, but the five furtive encounters in my sexual experiences dossier had all left me feeling repulsed and loathing myself. In short, I had a dreadful self-concept and suffered from a bad case of internalized homophobia.

That is where I was coming from on January 3, 1967, as I walked up the stone steps, onto the ancient porch, and through the weathered door that had known thousands of comings and goings.

Fred hollered down the staircase, "We're in the attic. Come on up!"

My trepidation didn't lessen as I climbed the worn wooden steps. When I got to the door at the bottom of the attic stairs, three men were just starting their descent, maneuvering a huge, tattered fainting couch. Both of Fred's companions struck me as attractive men. I couldn't help but notice their physiques as they strained with their burden. When they finally reached the landing, they put down the couch. Fred gave me a knowing smile.

"I'm giving this old monster to Gary for his wife," he said. "Barry, meet George and Gary. Guys, this is my friend Barry."

The contrast in the two strangers' demeanors was striking. Gary, married and ostensibly straight, immediately turned me off with his bubbliness and effeminate mannerisms, such was the grip my homophobia had on me. George, on the other hand, intrigued me with his cool reserve. I was glad that Gary was the one about to drive off with the couch.

Although they had known each other since their school days and now worked together professionally, this was the first time George had been to Fred's home.

After Gary took off with his wife's treasure, the remaining three of us settled down in front of the fire in Fred's newly remodeled parlor. It was a truly beautiful restoration—just the first of many that Fred had planned for the house. The room was gaily decorated for the holidays. Fred's Christmas tree, a perfectly shaped blue spruce, was exquisitely adorned with antique ornaments and subdued white lights. It shared the corner with his stereo, so the music seemed to be emanating from the tree itself. Candles placed around the room made it easy to imagine being taken back in time. It was a perfect setting for quiet conversation.

It gradually dawned on me that Fred had frequently mentioned George to me without giving him a name. He was twenty-four, blond, stood slightly over six feet tall, had broad shoulders, a twenty-eight-inch waist, and large, strong hands. One of his eyes had a slight squint, giving him a rakish, piercing expression. His labors on his parents' dairy farm—plowing, baling hay and straw, and tending the herd—had given him a magnificent, muscular body. George certainly fit Fred's description of "this gorgeous young hunk at work who . . ." Of course, I knew there was no way imaginable that he would ever be interested in me.

By nature effusive, I've always been attracted to men who are bright, quiet, and reserved. So it didn't take long for me to be seriously turned on by George's laid-back, soft-spoken shyness and by his dry wit.

When the music ended, and while Fred was freshening our drinks, I decided to crawl behind the Christmas tree to replay Sinatra's *Strangers in the Night*. I loved the song. For months it had been impossible to go into a bar, gay or straight, and not hear it at least half a dozen times.

As I was concentrating on not breaking any of "mother's" heirloom tree ornaments, I felt a hand very purposefully massage my right bun. This from the quiet, unassuming George! The shock almost sent my head plowing into the wall. It was a miracle that I didn't bring the whole tree crashing down! As I slowly backed out and turned around, George had a twinkle in his eye and an expansive grin on his face. My gonads gave a leap and my heart did a flip.

After another hour of constantly replenished glasses, conversation, and Sinatra, Fred discreetly excused himself. First, however, he insisted that—because of the icy roads and because we had been drinking—George and I would have to stay the night. He was the very picture of innocence as he apologized for having only one habitable spare bedroom, what with the renovations and all.

To say I was nervous would be a monumental understatement. Fifteen minutes into a wonderfully relaxed conversation, George, without a word, gently took my hand and led me toward the stairway.

"Please, God," I thought, "just this once, don't let this be another fiasco!"

My stomach was in turmoil and my mind in utter chaos, but there seemed to be a pervasive sense of calm surrounding us, thanks to George's gentle, self-assured control of the situation. I simply followed George up the stairs, still holding his hand.

I knew that the house was difficult to heat, and that the guest bedroom was the worst. It was freezing in there! We could see our breath in the air. Of course, with my insecurity, I insisted that the room be dark.

George intuitively took the lead. Although actually two years my junior, George was emotionally many years my senior. I could tell that this new person in my life had learned to like himself just as he was. My mind was boggled, even as I reveled in his patience and gentleness. He must have sensed how inexperienced and uptight I was, because he seemed perfectly willing to limit our first encounter to hugging and kissing.

We stayed awake and talked till dawn, something that neither of us had ever done before. Given George's laconic nature, it's more than likely that I did most of the talking. That's impossible to prove since neither of us can recollect even one thing we talked about at such length throughout the night. What I can recall, though, is the feeling I had, hour after hour, of being both exhilarated and relaxed. Never before had I felt such comfortable sexual intimacy with another human being. I felt totally accepted just as I was. The sense of euphoria was something that I had never experienced before. For one lovely night, this man had totally distracted my attention away from my physical hang-ups. Imagine feeling free, even temporarily, of being a pariah?

The next day was a normal work day and I should have been tired, but I wasn't. The only thing I could do was mull over the events of the previous evening. Prior to this, once sex was over, that was it. Except for the guilt, of course. But for the first time, I didn't feel guilty about the disgusting thing I had done. My only thought was "How am I going to see this man again?"

Since I was going to move into a new apartment the following week, that evening I called George and asked him if he would be willing to help. His immediate "Sure!" sent me into a tizzy. The week dragged by. Our second meeting, when it finally took place, was just as positive as our first.

George helped me set up my new bed, and of course, we had to "break it in." Afterward, I took him to dinner at one of the local college bars. To this day he likes to kid me about how chintzy I was that I took him to a hamburger joint. What did I know about dating, not having done it before? I'm certain that I did most of the talking, and because I was on such a high, I must have charmed the hell out of George. He was only seeing one side, at this point, and wasn't aware of the green-eyed monster that was lurking behind my glib facade and was about to rear its ugly head.

Forty-three days after our first meeting, I received a Valentine's Day card in the mail. On the front stood a happy little cartoon fellow grinning from ear to ear and holding a quiver with four arrows sticking out, saying "Every time I think of you . . ." Inside the card, it read, "I get a little quiver." It was signed "Your New Lover." Your new lover? Your first lover. And who would have ever thought, your only lover throughout life. My immediate response was to call Fred to share my ecstasy.

Sexually, ours was a student-teacher relationship. And, boy, did I desperately need a teacher. I was ashamed of my body as well as what I was doing with it—and what I wasn't doing with it. One of the first lessons that I learned was that it was okay to have a light on and watch. It wasn't an easy lesson.

The greatest gift that George has given me has been to help me develop a sense of sexual well-being. Just by being himself, he taught me that it was okay to be myself. What an empowering lesson! It didn't happen overnight, of course, because I still had some personal demons to slay, but at least he was patiently showing me the way.

In the following months, I became the aggressor in our relationship, at least outside the bedroom. When we didn't see each other, I would call just to chit-chat and to be reassured that there was a person out there who cared about me in spite of my physical and sexual limitations. My feelings were so intense that all other aspects of my life faded in importance. If George had any imperfections or negative attributes, I couldn't see them. And because he seemed to be equally unaware of my many shortcomings, I was walking on air.

This period was hectic. Every sexual act that I had tried before, few as they were, took on a whole new meaning with George. Gradually I found myself wanting to try everything. In fact, each of the experiences new to my repertoire sent me into a frenzy of wanting to try a variation on the theme. I can vividly remember George laughing and saying, "Take your time, we'll get to everything. We have the rest of our lives."

After four months, there was no question in my mind that this was *it*. I assumed that he felt the same way. In my heart, I really felt that I loved this man enough to want to spend the rest of my life with him. I started becoming complacent and possessive. The arguing began. At times it was ferocious, at least on my part. After all, my parents had fought. Wasn't this what relationships were about?

I didn't see it happening, but I was becoming more and more hostile, hateful, nasty, vindictive, and above all else, jealous. If another man dared to even look at my man, I would start a fight. Inevitably, I earned a reputation as a viper.

With the benefit of over thirty years to reflect on the phenomenon, I've concluded that many gay people have so thoroughly internalized society's prevailing belief that "our kind" can't maintain a satisfactory relationship over the long haul, they unconsciously set themselves up for a self-fulfilling prophecy. Now I understand that all those years ago, while I desperately wanted a life with George, I did my best to make sure that I would never have it. I shudder at the memory of all the ugly scenes—minor and major, private and public—to which I subjected this poor, gentle man!

One of my earliest big mistakes revolved around my desire to provide my lover with new experiences. He had taught me so much that I felt driven to reciprocate. George had never been to a gay bar. Since I was an old hand, having visited one maybe half a dozen times, I decided it was time to initiate him. We went to the Golden Greeks, the only gay establishment in the area. Talk about opening Pandora's box!

Given George's great face, body, and intriguing personality, he had no trouble making contact with almost anyone in sight. What had I done? By the end of that first evening, written all over his face was the look of a very happy man who knew he had died and gone to heaven. My George became a Golden Greeks regular whenever I wasn't around.

From the very beginning a huge source of contention and heartache was his need for an open relationship. That was something I definitely was not ready for, since I knew that anyone else he might see would, of course, be more desirable than me. It was obvious that I would have to be on my toes and guard my vested interest tooth and nail. One immediate result of my belligerent jealousy was to make it necessary for George to lie in order to cover his extramarital peccadilloes. *Oy*, could he lie! And because I wanted and needed to believe him, I did.

At the time we met, George was running with a couple of other men. He was up-front about it from the beginning. One was Jim, a man who worked for George's firm as a secretary. George told me that their liaison had been going on for five years and that Jim was ten years older than him. He tried to assure me that Jim was a harmless person, but I perceived him as a real threat. Not having met Jim, I could only imagine what an experienced gay man might have in what I figured must be his formidable bag of magical, sexual tricks.

One snowy evening we were at George's third-floor apartment. I was in a fantastic mood since it was obvious from the intensity of the storm that there wasn't going to be school the next day. Around midnight the phone rang. I answered it.

"Who the f--- are you? I'm coming the f--- over." I couldn't tell if it was a woman's voice or a drunkenly shrill man's. Shaking, I handed the phone to George.

He quietly but firmly told the caller to forget about coming over. The ensuing "Yes, I am!" "No, you are not!" went on for several minutes until George got fed up and slammed down the receiver.

I visualized an ominous shadow figure climbing the three flights of outside steps in the blizzard, banging on the door, bursting in, and slashing us both. George tried to reassure me that everything was all right. Of course, I wouldn't hear of it. I insisted that we leave and go to my apartment. Nothing George said could convince me that our lives weren't in imminent danger. After all, I had grown up in an inner-city ghetto, hadn't I? And hadn't I seen with my own eyes what havoc could flare up because of some romantic interloper? It didn't matter that George said that Jim was harmless. What did a farm boy know about such things?

Just to shut me up, we left. So swift was my flight that for the next week, as the snow melted on the outside steps and around his parking space, George kept finding bits and pieces of my dropped belongings.

When I finally met Jim about six months later at Fred's, I felt like a total jerk. George had been absolutely right in saying I had nothing to fear from this jovial, comedic, outrageous black queen who occasionally allowed alcohol and marijuana to control her mouth and her actions. Jim could easily have passed for a woman. (And when I say woman, I mean *w-o-m-a-n*! Later, after laughing about the whole affair, George and I dubbed Jim "Miss Thang.") She was stereotypical—almost a caricature—of a flighty drag queen. Tall and slim, Miss Thang carried herself delicately and demurely, always attempting to be prim and proper. She took small steps that gave her a gliding, feminine, swishing gait. Miss Thang almost made me look butch! If anything, I probably owe her a debt of gratitude. I'm certain that I benefited many times over from what she taught George.

I perceived a more serious threat as coming from Ed, a man that I had met. He was a class act. George was dwarfed by this 6'6", handsome, well-built, educated blond. Now this was competition. For a period of five months, Ed was George's Monday night trick. The fact that I had the need to drive by Ed's apartment to check on George's car tells the story of my sickness. How was my knowing for sure where he was going to change the situation? What it did was cause me further depression, hysterical overreacting, and teeth gnashing. In spite of constant reassurance from George that Ed represented nothing but fun and games and that I had nothing to worry about, I shed many uncontrollable and frenzied tears.

One of the worst scenes from that period took place after I caught George in a whopper of a lie. He told me that he was going to his parents', and as usual, I believed him. Actually, he had spent the weekend with Ed. I excitedly entered George's apartment Sunday evening to welcome him back from the farm. As he was unpacking, I found a program for *The Music Man* lying on the bed where he had inadvertently left it. I went berserk! I ranted and raved and acted like a fishwife. Not only were my feelings hurt, but this is what I feared most—the intimidation of another trespassing on my territory and shutting me out of George's life completely.

During this whole period, it was Fred's constant encouragement to be cool and hang in that got me through the turmoil, most of it of my own making.

It's small wonder that George began to weary of my almost constant abuse. He tried to be as honest as possible about his feelings, but I refused to hear. Finally he told me that, while he cared a great deal about me, he didn't know how much longer he would be able to tolerate my irrational outbursts. Even that veiled warning didn't soak in.

Looking back, I realize now that during that early period I was given to great, erratic mood swings. I could instantly go from a high so high that I couldn't think a negative thought if I had to, to a low so low that I would either withdraw in depression for days on end or become a suddenly venomous bitch.

The episode that brought things to a head occurred about ten months into our relationship. George once again was going to the farm for the weekend. Fred and I decided to go to the bar. Surprise! Surprise! One guess who was sitting at the bar when we walked in. I became hysterical and turned around and ran out, but only after every eye in the place was on me. Fred followed immediately and attempted in vain to console me.

In the morning Fred reported on his phone conversation with George after my melodramatic scene of the previous evening. He informed me that George was livid and that he didn't want to see me anymore. My hysterics in the bar had been the last straw. Through Fred I finally heard what George had been trying to tell me all along. The words were like an attention-getting punch to the solar plexus. I finally understood that if I wanted any kind of relationship with the man I loved so desperately, I was going to have to make drastic changes. Within a few days, once again through "mother's" blessed intercession, George begrudgingly agreed to give me one more chance.

Most assuredly, I did not change overnight, but I did make a concerted effort not to keep putting George on the spot. Normally, in checking on his comings and goings, I would interrogate him carefully as I attempted to set him up, and then, finding a discrepancy—no matter how small—I would pounce. Losing the Gestapo tactics was not easy, since I was striving to modify a behavior pattern of long standing. Although I occasionally backslid, I think George knew that I really was trying.

I tried to give my man some leeway in his outside sex life, but for myself I clung tenaciously to my own form of romanticism, which meant monogamy. A very probable second reason why I wasn't active myself during that time was because I never really enjoyed sex until George came along. Why bother going through the hassle if it was going to be bad anyhow?

Without question, I had to break the vicious cycle of insecurity, possessiveness, and jealousy. I told myself over and over that just because my husband wanted a little "piece of strange" once in a while, it didn't mean the end of what we had going for us. The big lesson that I was learning, and wouldn't incorporate for a while, was that the fidelity of my relationship was based on emotional commitment and not sexual exclusivity.

During this period of my studied self-analysis and rehabilitation, we gradually began to merge our two individualities into one new entity. My desire to merge was definitely greater than George's, but he was coming along. We were still in the process of our mutual learning-about-you phase, of course. I suppose we both felt that, given time, we would be able to change those little things that grated on each other's nerves. We had yet to learn that there are certain traits and habits that every couple has to accept in each other and learn to deal with. "For better or worse, till death do us part."

George must have been impressed with my progress, because in October 1968, twenty-one months after we met, we decided to live together. We set up housekeeping in a third-floor, two-bedroom, ninety-dollars-a-month apartment.

As I continued to work toward gaining confidence in myself, and as George worked toward tolerating the verbal abusiveness that the vestiges of my internalized homophobia still occasionally ignited, the intensity and content of our disagreements started to subtly change. The bulk of our disagreements revolved around the so-called Oscar-Felix syndrome. I am basically a slob, and although George may have a different point of view, to which he is certainly entitled, to me he was, is, and will probably always remain a "clean queen" personified. Like my mother, may she rest in peace, I have never been bothered by a little *schmutz* (dirt). For me, the floor was a receptacle for whatever I didn't want in my hand if a wastebasket or table wasn't convenient. For George, everything has its proper place, and nothing is to be disturbed without incurring his displeasure. As with most areas of disparity and discord in a relationship, compromise has to take place at some time if the affiliation is to continue on an even keel. In our case, over time I improved dramatically, and George bent a trifle. Again, my mate would probably disagree vociferously. At present, I am allowed to keep a pile or two around if it doesn't get too offensive or out of hand. When George really becomes offended visually, he will give me fair warning.

"If those piles aren't gone in two days, I'm shoving them into a bag and putting them into your closet." True to his word, after two days of ignoring his warnings, I inevitably come home to a neat floor and a cluttered closet. It works for us.

We also began exposing each other to our varied interests, backgrounds, and lifestyles. George, for instance, introduced me to a whole new world of horticulture. For my part I suggested that we go to New York since he had never been there. Except for that infamous production of *The Music Man*, which we both chose to forget, he had never seen a musical; so we were both enthralled by Pearl Bailey in *Hello Dolly!* The dimly lit nude scene in the scandalous musical *Hair* provided us with a story for back home. I couldn't believe that someone George's age could have gone through life without having eaten Chinese food. With his first bite he was a convert.

On the whole, though, George didn't enjoy our trip as much as I did. While the jaunt had its memorable moments, without even a minor argument to spoil it, the hustle and bustle of the Big Apple turned him off. He was still a farm boy at heart.

My first trip to my "in-laws," home took place on a crisp, early fall Sunday afternoon. They lived on a 200-acre dairy farm. The corn on either side of their long, dirt lane had recently been harvested and the only thing left was the bent stalks. As we drove up to the two-story, white-frame house, the chicken and ducks were sent skittering around the yard. The only creature that didn't run as we approached was Ginger, a friendly, lumbering, Chesapeake Bay retriever. Around the kitchen porch, late flowers still bloomed in profusion. The only plants I could identify at the time were the roses. I was visiting a whole new world, and I was totally fascinated. The small vegetable garden, although past its peak, was still producing its beans, tomatoes, and squash, none of which I had ever seen on the vine.

George's father, tall and broad, was a jovial, outgoing gentleman. His mother was friendly but very reserved. I immediately could see that George was very much his mother's son. All of George's family—his four older sisters, an older brother, and their children—had gathered for a day in the country. All the siblings were married and had moved to populated areas that were within driving distance. After the introductions, George took me on a tour of the barn.

The Holstein cows were being brought in after spending the day grazing in the fields. I was amazed at how each cow knew exactly which stall to enter. George's nephew was sweeping the gutter behind the cows. It was at this point that George gave me a crash course in bovine behavior.

"When you see a cow raise her tail," George told me with a grin, "make sure you're not standing behind her."

At that precise moment, as if to demonstrate the lesson, one of the cows did, indeed, raise its tail. I gaped in amazement. The milking machine was tugging at one of her teats after another as the white fluid was spurting into the container. Bossy looked at me with her gentle eyes as she contentedly chewed her cud, seemingly oblivious to the precious fluid the machine was taking from her and without the least trace of embarrassment at the fact that she was giving a city boy his first view of a cow creating a major cow pie. I couldn't believe the amount of steaming, streaming stench that shot out of the orifice under her raised tail. She shot me a final, disdainful look, let her tail fall, switched it back and forth a time or two, then smugly lowered her face into the feeding trough. In the midst of all this, I heard a bell clanging. It was George's mother announcing dinner.

After dinner, fifteen of us went for a walk in one of the farm's many wooded areas. As we were crossing a small, narrow gully, everyone suddenly let out a whoop and started running in all directions. Instead of joining the rest of the crowd in their retreat, I took a few more steps forward to see what had caused their panic. Looking down to see what was causing the strange humming noise at my feet, I saw the first of what immediately turned into a swarm of very dangerous insects. I was terrified, and I started running too late! We had stumbled onto a nest of yellow jackets. After it became obvious that I wasn't going to have an allergic reaction after being stung thirty times, everybody thought the episode was quite funny, particularly George's mother. Everybody, that is, except me! To this day, thirty-odd years later, if you ever want to know what a real screaming sissy looks and sounds like, let me notice a flying insect within four feet of me.

As the years started to roll by, as George and I continued our merging, we also grew as individuals. I had my separate interests and friends, and George had his. I finally understood that George's desire to be his own person was not meant as a rejection of me as a person.

Once I was well into my recovery, our relationship became like that of any other "normal" couple. We worked together to achieve our tacit, mutual goal: to make our lives as productive and enjoyable as we could. After the first two years, there was no longer "mine" and "yours." It was "ours." Of course, we had our misunderstandings, but we were able to work things through by talking and compromising.

Thank goodness, finances have never caused any dissension between us. Our salaries have always been comparable, so there has never been any rivalry. We also share the same philosophy on spending: If we can't pay for something (other than a house or a car) in thirty days, then we don't need it.

And so our life finally became idyllic. It remained that way until year sixteen.

For six months I had the all-pervasive feeling that something was wrong between George and me. There wasn't any fighting or arguing about anything major or even minor. The tumultuous times spent on getting our act together as a couple were behind us. Things were going along effortlessly and smoothly. We had reached a point where friendship and companionship were the mainstays of our relationship. So why this feeling that something was wrong?

I had finally become so secure in our relationship, perhaps I had started taking for granted what I had. Now I started missing all the little cutesy things—the hugging and the kissing and the general playfulness—that were no longer there. I'm not talking about sex, because that really wasn't that important at this point. It slowly dawned on me that I was bored with my existence. Was that the cause of the malaise and overall sadness that I felt so often? Was this all there would ever be? I had everything to be thankful for, and yet I was despondent. There were actually days when I didn't want to leave work because of the tension I felt at home. What was wrong with me? Things could not go on like this.

It had been years since I had had to take a Valium before one of our "communication sessions," but I knew it was time for one again.

I explained to George exactly how I felt. My basic premise was that I didn't need a room-mate, that I could very easily live a contented life on my own. He agreed with me and admitted that he was having precisely the same feeling. We recognized that sixteen years was a long time, and since we were friends and truly cared a great deal about each other, we would make a concerted effort to try to get back to where we had been. If we could do it, fine; if not, we'd deal with the ramifications when the time came.

A fascinating aspect of all this was our major concern: If things didn't work out, how would our friends handle all of this? After sixteen years of "wedded bliss," we were unquestionably held up as role models. I knew that I certainly wasn't prepared to deal with their reactions to our breakup. We agreed not to discuss our difficulties with anyone, not even Fred.

Our first major attempt at rejuvenating our relationship was to plan a trip to Europe for the following summer. George decided, since he had never been abroad, that he wanted to see London, Paris, and Rome. And since I had visited all three, I could be his own resident expert. I really didn't care where we went, as long as we went together! Our preparations were almost as exciting as the trip was going to be. We sent for passports, bought new clothes, obtained small amounts of currency from each of the countries we would be visiting, and read all the literature we could find about the various sights. It was amazing how often famous European landmarks appear in television commercials and movies once we felt a vested interest. Notre Dame seemed to pop up once or twice a week. Whenever there was even a fleeting glimpse of a place we would be visiting, I'd let out an excited high-pitched shriek that would scare the bejesus out of poor George.

Each completed task was a step closer to the trip we thought of as our second honeymoon and fueled our anticipation. Although life in general seemed to be speeding by at a new whirlwind pace, it also seemed as if departure day would never arrive. We were both so swept up in our adventure that we had forgotten that we were supposed to be on the verge of "divorce."

In August 1984, after buying our fifth of duty-free Tanqueray gin, we boarded a Boeing 747, a new experience for both of us. I have never been able to sleep on a plane, and our shared excitement all but guaranteed that this flight would be no exception. The jet lag would be a bitch, but what the hell. We could always catch up on sleep when we got home.

The highlight of the trip had nothing to do with where we were or what we saw. It had everything to do with George. The special moment ranks right up there with the night we met.

We had done London. We had done Paris. We had done Rome. Now, on my forty-fourth birthday, we were nearing the end of our trip. We were driving along the Appian Way on the way to Florence.

"By the way," George said quietly, "when we get to the jewelry factory in Florence, I'd like to buy us a pair of matching rings."

"I beg your pardon," I said incredulously.

"You heard me. I want to buy a set of matching rings for us."

"After all these years, you've finally decided to make an honest woman out of me? Well, what do you know?" This from a man who is basically a nonromantic.

Très romantique, n'est-ce pas?

Yes! We were definitely going to be okay!

Since year sixteen, there has been a quality of excitement and romance in our life together that hadn't existed for a long time. Certainly the frequency of sex has declined over the years, but it has been more than compensated for by an abundance of open tenderness, affection, and closeness. There is a sense of peace, contentment, and security, with feelings of permanence and a lack of loneliness. There has been a renewal of the simple pleasure found in just being together. The love that we possess today is not the love that got us started. Without question, it is an all-encompassing love that is stronger and more durable; a love without the friction and consternation, a love that has made getting

up everyday a sheer joy. We have finally learned that, basically, the only truly important thing we have in our lives is each other. Also, we still have the ability to make each other laugh.

Life trundled along joyously until December 1991. George, with a total of thirty years, had planned to retire in June 1991. I was becoming a little weary of his telling me how he was going to sleep late while I had to work five more years. However, midway through the year, there were rumblings that in order to save the state money, the governor was considering an early retirement plan. By March 1991, it was a fait accompli. If an employee had twenty-five years of service, the state would give him or her credit for five years in order to retire. I had not experienced the same state of euphoria since that fateful night when I had my first encounter with my husband on January 3, 1967! I never stopped to consider how much I was going to get, I just asked, "Where do I sign?" I figured my accountant husband would handle all the details! I retired first by fifteen days. I was fifty and he was forty-nine. A new phase of our lives began.

On the last day of June I went into school to pick up my last paycheck of my work career and to say goodbye to all my friends. When I got home the phone was ringing. It was the manager of the local newspaper.

"Congratulations!! We're having a promotion to celebrate our 150th anniversary and you've won a seven-day cruise on the Mexican Riviera."

For once I was speechless. If this is any indication of what our retirement is going to be like, *oy vey*!

Today, George hasn't lost a bit of his special ability to keep me at once both exhilarated and relaxed. It seems impossible that it has been thirty-two years since that night we met and he provided me with the first positive sexual experience of my life. Now we know each other so well that it's hard to remember even that I once had a life without him.

"Old Blue Eyes" had it exactly right about strangers in the night.

Frederick Schram and

Brian Kirkpatrick

-eleven-

behind the glass wall

B R I A N   K I R K P A T R I C K

Icannot imagine what the tourists think staring through our kitchen windows. We, my lover and I, live on a major canal in Amsterdam, and the apartment we own has two floors, a lower level, the *souterrain* in Dutch, and the ground floor (five steps above the sidewalk), which the Dutch call the *bel etage*, denoting our twelve-foot decorated ceilings and a pair of nine-foot windows that face the seventeenth-century facades on the other side of the canal. People passing by our kitchen stop and bend over slightly. They gawk. They point. One group of Italian tourists videotaped my lover at the sink preparing dinner, no doubt thinking that they had captured a typical middle-aged Dutch husband. Another time, a tourist photographed our green garbage bags on the sidewalk. Our neighbors in the building—there are five apartments—pause to inhale the fumes from my stews, and once, when Fred and I were at a restaurant around the corner, the manager approached, introduced herself, and said that she noted the daily change in our fruit bowl.

It's taken a few years to adjust to all this attention. Fred and I would prefer a more private existence. Fred, especially, does not look forward to the mornings when he scuffs back and forth in front of the window in his bathrobe. But we live with the eyes upon us. Figuring out how to install blinds around the water pipes suspended from the ceiling, the old beams, and the exhaust duct that vents through a pane of glass is beyond our imagination. Lately, I have begun to look back at those who peek, and if I am in a decent mood, I will nod. This can startle the voyeurs. In the summer, tour boats pass every ten minutes, and if I happen to be standing in front of our living room window, watering plants, for instance, people will wave. I do not wave back.

No one has ever seen anything smutty looking in. Once, just once, when we had a French schoolteacher visiting, we were a bit high from the Belgian beer he had brought, but we made sure that when we peeled our zippers, we were well below the island that separates the kitchen from the dining area and so out of view.

American visitors are giddy with the range of sex available in Amsterdam, with the municipal tolerance, with the novel zoning idea that a city should set aside areas specializing in sex as well as museums. But, in a strange way, the fact that Amsterdam has tax-paying prostitutes, male and female, is related to our kitchen windows with no blinds or curtains. Dutch tradition maintains that almost anything is permissible as long as it is out in the open. Thus, for centuries, in Dutch cities and villages, there has been a custom that the view through windows facing the street (meaning the living room ones) remains unobstructed for the neighbors to look in. Of course, in the late twentieth century, with burglaries and strangers moving about, this custom is observed less and less. We close our living room drapes though only after an hour or two of darkness.

If tourists can sate their curiosity about how people live in a canal house, Fred and I benefit, too, looking out. We have seen the most shocking and pleasurable sights in the windows of the hotel across the way. Businessmen with their morning erections excited about the Amsterdam rooftops. Plus we see an endless parade of headless crotches and torsos from our vantage point inside. Especially with daylight savings time gone, those on the sidewalk can see, in the lamplight every night between 5:30 and 6:30, two middle-aged gay men eating their dinner. In a weird way, we fit perfectly into this culture because we, like most Dutch families, like to eat early.

We are here in Amsterdam because my lover, Frederick Schram, was appointed to the chair of the department of systematics and biogeography at the University of Amsterdam in 1992. His specialty is shrimps, crabs, and lobsters, living and fossil varieties, in other words, the evolution of those succulent creatures. Our American visitors don't quite grasp Fred's high visibility, nor do they recognize the tensions that come with the position.

Fred is a *hoogleraar* B, which is Dutch civil service jargon for head professor. To our surprise, we discovered that the title impressed the bank manager when we sat down with her to open our accounts, and later, when we checked with her about a mortgage, she offered a sum well beyond what we intended to spend because of Fred's tenured, civil servant position. Once, as I toured apartments with our *makelaar* (real estate agent), he dismissed what I thought was a promising place by saying, "A *hoogleraar* does not enter his building through the basement."

In Fred's particular situation, he supervises the teaching and research of the entire zoology staff; he sits on national committees; participates in never-ending reorganizations; prods graduate students to write their theses—all in a foreign language he did not know five years ago. In addition, he receives foreign scientists for lunch and tours of the institute whether the visitors study beetles or caribou; represents his institute in EU-sponsored networks around Europe; writes and delivers scientific papers; and when he retires in twelve years, he will, as his four predecessors did, have his portrait painted. (We joke that he should pose in his black leather jacket.) Finally, up until a few years before Fred arrived, the position was considered of such importance that the contract required the queen's signature.

I mention Fred's duties to give an indication of how much he and our relationship are on display. We live in a glass box. How two working-class American guys like ourselves wound up here keeps our families mystified. They have never lived more than a hundred miles from where they were born, in Chicago and Connecticut, and some are afraid to fly.

Fred and I met in San Diego in January 1987. Fred had recently separated from his wife (his teenage son remained with her), and he had just begun exploring his gay side. I, on the other hand, had had fifteen years of relationships and affairs. My life back in Boston had reached a stalemate. I was about to put aside my third unsuccessful novel. I had been stopped at night on the streets of Dorchester twice, once by guns and once by knives. I was unable to find a lover or just a compatible roommate. Finally, a tarot reader told me that I would be much happier once I moved to the West Coast. A lover was out there waiting and a new life, too. The cards, however, did not specify a city and so, after saving for a year, working seven days a week as a housecleaner, I sat down with a travel agent, and we scheduled a month-long trip through four cities.

I arrived in San Diego in October 1986. It was drizzling when I pulled up to my hotel. I

121

opened the door of the rented car and my lungs filled with the scent of eucalyptus. That sold me. Only two days there, but it was enough. The sweet, warm smell was the signal I had sought. I went on for two more weeks, first to L.A., then San Francisco, knowing already that I had found my place.

I returned to Boston, packed my furniture and books, put them all in storage, then bought a one-way ticket to San Diego. By December, I was living in a motel, with some clothes, my typewriter, a rented car, and enough savings, if I lived modestly, to carry me through the following year. On my second day, in a coffee shop eating breakfast, I met Matthew, who offered to rent me his spare bedroom. Back in Boston, the tarot had told me not to worry about where I would live. That if I set out, my home would materialize. And indeed, it did on my second day. A few weeks later, with Matthew's help, I bought a futon and a bleached maple trestle table for my typewriter, then I turned in my rented car.

In the middle of January, I was ready to find my lover. I composed the following personal ad and submitted it to the local gay weekly:

FONDLE MY PAWS

Regal, creative Leo (my age, weight, etc.) stalking compatible mate. Be someone, 35–50, who is not intimidated by bedroom purring or agile mind.

Fred's response appeared in my rented mailbox a few days later. He signed it with only his first name and his box number. I wrote back. We talked on the phone for an hour and a half, discovered that we lived within a fifteen-minute walk of each other, and we both admitted that we had not eaten dinner yet. So we met halfway at City Deli, talked another hour. We dated once or twice. He was extremely busy at the time as acting director of the San Diego Natural History Museum. He had been curator of paleontology for twelve years. Two weeks passed before we landed on my futon.

In my passport, the Dutch immigration police note my relationship with Fred. I am allowed to live here as his gay partner, even though we are both Americans, because Fred has a work permit for a tenured appointment. An immigration policeman wrote out the terms of my residence. It takes up a whole page of my passport. I am not allowed to work, and if we should ever split up, Fred—not the Dutch government—is responsible for buying me a plane ticket home. The Dutch do not want me on their welfare roles. That we are a gay couple has never caused so much as a tightened lip among the countless Dutch we have dealt with whether we are at the bank, the hospital, or city hall. Once we make clear we are a couple, people move ahead with the task at hand.

There was never any question in Fred's mind that we had taken this adventure together. He had been downsized out of the San Diego Museum, and he began a search for a museum directorship across America on the strength of his administrative experience, his textbooks, and his research. Over a period of two years, he applied, in not any particular order, for positions in Albany, Seattle, Albuquerque, Milwaukee, Lancaster, and Bozeman. We might have landed in any of those places.

The business of being a dependent spouse I did not swallow easily. I had always paid my own way, and although I had not accumulated any savings during the years I had been writing part-time, I paid my rent and health insurance. I never owned a car. In America, we had cemented our emotional relationship, but we had kept our money separate. Looking back, I realize that I viewed financial dependence (and the security it offered) as a trap. Not only had I never expected to own property, the idea made me queasy. So, too, did pension funds. Planning for retirement, indeed, seemed a bit odd since my writing career, at mid-life, has not even taken off. I had a lot of ego to swallow.

On the second day of Fred's work in Amsterdam, his secretary asked us to sign a form.

"Consider yourselves married," she said. The form was for the *Belastingdienst* (the Dutch IRS), and with it, Fred could claim an exemption for me on his salary.

As with most stay-at-home spouses, I cook, clean, and market in between my writing. Sometimes I deal with the plumber, especially if he comes with an assistant named Nico with size 25 neck and thighs like a sequoia trunk. Because of Fred's position at the university, we do a vast amount of entertaining, usually one or two foreigners at a time, sometimes with their wives: Russians, Brazilians, Chinese, Italians, Irish, Danes, both senior scientists and graduate students. I spend three hours in the streets with my shopping cart then, the next day, another six hours making my soup stock, appetizers, and so forth. I cook because I enjoy it, because I have accumulated recipes I want to share. I stage-manage a dinner party like a play. By the time the guests arrive, I am nervous, irritable, ready for a fight, and Fred, sometimes, expects the worst. "Have more sherry," he'll say.

A few times he has seen me walk out on guests. If there is one kind that makes my blood boil, it is the straight male scientist who eats my food and talks science the whole evening as if I were invisible. But most straight men, with or without their wives or women friends, delight in the domesticity Fred and I create, the nurturing aspect of our home life, and want to be part of it, to partake of my homemade soups as well as our aggressively affectionate cat, Bruno. Strangely, they each feel proud of having been accepted by Bruno as if our cat, somehow, were the final arbiter of who gets to stay and who gets asked to leave.

Most of the scientists, I daresay, have never been in such an intimate situation with gay men. If they are given a tour of our apartment, they will see the big barge of a bed which we (Fred, Bruno, and I) use for both TV watching and sleeping. And they might notice, among the bookcases, drawings, Persian tiles, and photos, the occasional object featuring men with erect cocks, a Mexican fertility idol, the vase done by an Amsterdam ceramicist, the calendar over my desk with the porn star Steve Kelso. This is who we are. We are not coy about it. We do not turn pictures toward the wall.

Fred's female colleagues, the ones who pass through Amsterdam, are dynamic, ambitious women with scientist husbands—career women without time for children and, thus, part of an adult couple like ourselves. They, too, can appreciate what it would be like to have a spouse at home making the appetizers.

If the scientist is here for more than two days, Fred will offer to take him or her on a walking tour of the city. If these visitors have seen Amsterdam, Fred offers a day trip to Delft or Haarlem. Sometimes I join. It's surprising how many people are taken by the slower pace of these provincial cities.

All this entertaining, while necessary, spawns invitations. A month in China, several weeks in Australia, a week in Brazil. People are anxious to get Fred's ear, and they are willing to pay his airfare and hotel. Lately, I have relaxed my sometimes rigid approach to writing, and I have accompanied Fred. Beyond the obvious opportunities to travel, I imagine we must trigger some consciousness-raising when the congress organizers are told that Fred and his male partner are coming. They must arrange or suggest sleeping accommodations, banquet seating as well as informal socializing, and as we travel, we rarely find a biologist who is out to us. No one, for instance, to admire with us the tantalizing, silky trousers of the gaucho dancer in Porto Alegre, Brazil, who stomped the floor and flicked two rope whips. After our guests leave, we blow out the candles, wash the wine glasses, read the day's paper and mail at 11 P.M. The lair is ours again.

I am sometimes troubled by how self-contained we have become, Fred, Bruno, and myself, the predictability of where we are in the apartment and what we are doing according to the clock. At 7:50 A.M., I pass Fred in the upstairs hall. He is emerging from the bathroom, dressed already, and I am heading downstairs in my bathrobe to brew tea and feed the cat. And, at the other end of the day, around 9 P.M., Fred or I roll down the bedspread to the floor, we fix our pillows so we can sit up either to read or to watch television, but only after we have made one last trip to the kitchen for cookies and one or the other has made a dash to the toilet, and only after the dust has settled and we are sprawled down each side of the bed does Bruno, who has been patiently sitting in the dark living room, saunter into the bedroom and with a small screech leap onto the bed.

In our craving for comfort among these daily rituals, we are not unlike our friends in London, Fred and John, our adopted uncles, who have been together for sixty-one years. In their eighties now, they pad around their lair, a warren of rooms that desperately need new walls, never mind paint. The landlord waits for them to die. They live on the second floor. Below them, the old woman died and the landlord quickly boarded up the windows. Above, the neighborhood council temporarily places immigrant families from the latest war zones in Africa or Asia. The neighborhood teeters. But inside their apartment, between 11 A.M. and noon, every day, Fred and John have Teacher's Hour in their living room. One or two glasses of Scotch as they wallow in their memories, many going back to the Second World War.

I suspect that my Fred and I cleave to our structured days because so much seems beyond our control or understanding. On a particular day, my imagination can be agreeable or not, the writing of a story or a chapter in my current novel might move forward or stall. A household emergency can erupt out of nowhere. Water damage is never far from our minds here in the Netherlands, whether it might come from the small pump that pushes the flow from our basement level up to the level of the sewer pipes (we have replaced it three times in three years) or from the relentless rains that pound the walls and windows of this 380-year-old building. Even Bruno participates by peeing on anything plastic or cardboard we leave on the floor. One popular Dutch torture in centuries past was to tie someone to a sub-basement wall and start filling the room with water. I know the fear well as I sit here at my computer below street level.

Fred braces every morning for what he terms "brush fires." He must dampen some people's ambitions and ignite others'. This being such a small country, there is not much room for egos, including Fred's. The Education Ministry loves to reorganize, pit one university against another, arrange shotgun marriages between research groups that have little in common, and by so doing politically try to force scientists from different disciplines to work together. The government pays all the bills, including the tuition and living stipends for students, and so it becomes a matter of outmaneuvering their grand plans.

Like our uncles in London, we, too, have a drinks hour, though not every day and definitely not in the morning. When Fred arrives home on his bicycle, I wave to him from the kitchen sink. If what I am making is complicated, I will suggest that he pour himself some port or Scotch, and he will stand on the other side of the island counter. A chance for us to relate our battles that day. But we are not left in peace. Bruno, bless his tail, is above us yowling and circling the living room, where he expects us at that hour for his pre-dinner petting. So we grab our glasses and the platter of appetizers and head up the stairs.

We don't see our uncles more than once or twice a year. But we exchange letters, and Fred and I have established a ritual of calling them on the first Sunday of the month between Teacher's Hour and the end of lunch, when they head to their separate bedrooms for a nap. Neither of them has any family still alive, and except for Nellie across the back alley, their friends are dead too. We ask about their health and they are anxious to tell us about the weather.

London Fred has a vast reservoir of smutty jokes, frequently about farting and the war effort in southern Italy, a talent for both remembering and telling these stories that proved invaluable during the decades he worked, first as a clerk, then as head buyer at Fortnum and Mason, the food emporium. Politicians and aristocrats would stop at the store, grab Fred's elbow, and hustle him to a quiet corner where they hoped he would have a joke or two they could tell at lunch. Fred could recommend a wine or pass on a story about a thirteen-inch cock—all with a smile and discretion. John spent his working years as a groom in private men's clubs. Two working blokes who picked up quite a few secrets.

They have said to us several times that they are glad they have lived in the closet. Not that their lives were uneventful. They enjoyed escapades in the military, in Piccadilly bars and public toilets. John will remember something from the 1930s, start giggling, and when he catches his breath, he will tell about a police bar raid and how he and his friends crawled out a basement window, or he will remember a lesbian friend, a tall, imperious woman, who would promenade through parties and the streets with short John and act as his protection.

To us, Fred and John are heroes, two gay men who have survived together for more than sixty years without being poisoned by bitterness. They have educated themselves through travel and books. In fact, they met my Fred on a cruise on the Nile in 1970s. And they will end their lives as they started, without a quid to their names.

Fred and I, feeling both harassed and exhilarated by the pace of our life, daydream occasionally about our retirement. We will have lived outside the United States for at least fifteen years at that point. We even ask Bruno if he will mind a flight, although of course the cat will no longer be alive. Neither will our uncles. Once, as we were leaving the uncles' apartment and exchanging hugs, I noticed that London Fred's eyes were teary. He told us that our departure made him feel as if the circus were leaving town. I imagine that we will feel the same way when we hear of their deaths.

Wherever we live in the States, Fred and I will establish a new lair. The move will be traumatic, because both of us are cautious in new places, me probably more than Fred with my agoraphobia striking at unpredictable moments. We expect to stay in this apartment until Fred retires, burrowing deeper and deeper like our uncles do in theirs. If we accumulate enough money, we hope to find a house that will provide us with two studies. That's our dream. We joke about needing two kitchens, at least two counters with their own sinks, but that goal has receded since we have learned from years of knocking into each other that it's best when only one of us is in the kitchen at a time. We run our kitchen on a time-share basis.

But it's much harder to do that with a space meant for intellectual privacy, isolation, quiet. Both in San Diego and in Amsterdam, we divided up the second bedroom into territories, *his* desk, *my* desk. In fact, in this apartment, we have a five-foot bookcase and our filing cabinets jutting out into the middle of the room like the Berlin Wall. In the ten years we been together, maybe five times have we tried to occupy the same thinking space. We're uncomfortable, conscious of the other person. By being generous, by deferring to the other the use of our one computer, we can rupture the work on our own project.

There are issues, explosive ones, that will never be resolved between Fred and me. My estrangement from his son, for instance, or conflicts over food and cleaning that tap into our childhoods, or Fred's passivity in the face of my depressions. Issues so hot I dare not enter them into this computer. They are there, but not open for discussion. The best we can do is to avoid touching the open wounds and hope that a few more decades together will heal them.

On one of our visits to London, we were in our uncles' living room enjoying a pre-lunch Scotch when Johnny disappeared for a few minutes. He returned with a cardboard folder, one with smudges and tape tears.

"I've got something," John said.

He settled down again on the sofa, licked his lips, and opened the back flap. He pulled out naughty drawings, 8.5 inches by 6.5, done with pen and watercolor.

"Where'd you get these?"

"Well, there was a bar called Prophet Corners Cafe," Johnny began. We established that it was 1931. John was about eighteen. An older man was showing these drawings to selected patrons. When John saw them, he knew he had to have them. And so he negotiated a night of sex for the set.

After we had examined them for a quite a few minutes, John put them back in the envelope and handed them to me. "They're yours now," he said.

I can't remember which excited me more, receiving the pictures or hearing John reminisce about London bar life in the early thirties. At the time, he was a valet at the Junior Naval and Military Club. I asked my Fred to get a pen, and he took notes on the front of the gray folder. The bar names and addresses (as much as John could remember), and the reasons he went to each.

Another time, John and Fred confided that they felt awkward with the word "gay." "Queer" was what they had always called themselves. As I sometimes do, I passed on information from the outside world. "Queer" was again in vogue among certain members of our community. I asked if they would ever consider being in the London Gay Pride march.

"Oh, no," Fred said, "our legs are no good for that."

I meant, of course, the two of them seated in a white Cadillac convertible as I had seen in the States with a big banner announcing their years of commitment.

"Well . . . ," John thought. The glamour certainly intrigued him even though, if offered the chance, he would never dare do it.

It's good for Fred and me to hear our uncles talk about sex, to hear, on the one hand, how male bodies decline and fail and to hear, too, how the libido lives on. Aside from the trips to the High Street for supplies and newspapers, and occasional cab rides to the doctor, the pensioners live among their plants, souvenir plaques and tiles, candy dishes and ashtrays.

When we find the time, Fred and I plan to have John's erotic drawings bound in leather. Attach a note about John and Fred, a few words about how they passed them on to us, perhaps a sentence or two about who we are. Then, when we reach our eighties, we will pass the volume on to a younger gay couple, and by so doing, keep alive the thrill of that night in 1931.

Last April, Fred and I revisited Florence. For eight days we clinked wine glasses and water goblets. We clinked plastic cups, soda cans, and capfuls of Pepto Bismol. Every half hour one of us was saying "Happy Anniversary." We bought ourselves matching black sweaters, cotton gossamer spun by a Florentine spider, and as appropriate for ten years together, we reached for sweaters a size larger than where we started.

I found enormous pine cones in Il Giardino dei Semplici (Cosimo I's botanical garden) and took a few back to the Hotel Porta Rossa. I put them on the top of the bureau. Each day I brought back a small pile. More pine cones from Siena. Snail shells. A tree knot big as a grapefruit. Chestnuts and seeds.

All the treasures I wrapped carefully. I tucked them in my luggage and brought them back to our apartment, or is it a nest? I searched a whole day in Amsterdam for the right vase—wide enough to accommodate the biggest cones, tall enough to display the entire collection. And so, inside that glass column, I arranged my anniversary bouquet, cheap enough, a feast for both the eyes and the fingers. Splinters from Florence to decorate our nest.

Joël Sartorius

and Robert Melucci

-twelve-

celebrating love

ROBERT C. MELUCCI AND JOËL SARTORIUS

JOËL

Bob and I have been together almost twenty-one years.

I was born on Halloween 1947, the product of a Jewish mother with an Eastern European ghetto worldview and a godless, Reform Jewish father with distinguished Confederate roots. Before I was three years old, I hoped to spend the rest of my life with Mason, the brother of my sister's playmate.

My parents were introverted and eccentric. My playmates were girls. My role model was cultured Aunt Marion, with whom I spent as much time as possible. The boys called me sissy. And I could never live up to my impatient, jock father's manliness expectations. It hurt to be shamed for loving "feminine things." Overall, life was a confusing circus. It was not difficult to lose myself in hopes that a knight on a dashing steed would carry me away from this troubled world.

Until eighteen, I was unaware that my attraction to men was homosexuality. Bonding with some of my cohorts in the ballet world was the beginning of the long, slow process toward understanding and appreciating my attraction to men. It was a pleasure to let myself go in the promiscuous gay 1970s. During college and graduate school I met many men, always hoping that one was the beginning of that lifelong relationship. After ending a two-year tempestuous relationship, I resolved to remain free. And then I met Bob.

BOB

I arrived in May 1941, a bit of a surprise to my parents, since my youngest sister was graduating from high school that very week. My brother was married at the time. His wife lived with us while he served in World War II in the Army Air Corps. Some of my earliest memories involve one of my two sisters rocking me to sleep when the blackout sirens sounded. My family was nominally Catholic, but anticlerical, although I do have pleasant memories of the Methodist Sunday school that my brother's wife took me to on occasion.

My father was a quiet but loving man, a heavy smoker who died of lung cancer when I was seven. I have fond memories of the walks we took together after supper each evening. My mother was also loving but made of sterner stuff, which she made sure you respected. I knew to obey her, but also became aware that I was far less afraid of her than my sisters and brother were.

Although I did not care much for competitive sports during these early years (but did ask my brother to send me a doll from France, which he did), I always appeared masculine. I have no recollection of being called a sissy. I first became aware of my attraction to males in high school. Although I did not have any gay friends, my mother let me know at the age of eighteen that being gay was all right. She often took me to art films and filmed operas. After one Italian film she explained a brothel scene where a man went off with a younger man. In Europe this behavior was acceptable, yet something Americans were too naive to understand. I realized she was discussing more than the film. During college I knew of some gay bars but did not relate to the people who frequented them. I decided to wait until college was over. Actually, I was too busy working and going to school to think of much else.

After college I made up for lost time and met many men. Just after graduate school and during my first years of teaching college I had my first long-term relationship. It lasted eight years. However, I was still young and became restless. Parting was difficult. But Tom and I remained good friends. Alas, barhopping was not my cup of tea, and I soon found myself in another relationship, a complete disaster. Shortly thereafter I met Joël.

JOËL

I had expected to meet my forever companion in some dreamily romantic site, our eyes locking across a crowded room. The room was crowded, but it was in a smoky bar. I stood eating popcorn, which I had jokingly loaded into an empty brandy snifter. I looked up to notice nearby a man who was my physical ideal. He looked foreign enough that I wondered what language he spoke. He seemed reserved. I feared he would have no interest in me. Did I look too desperate? By and by our seriousness gave way to relaxed, shy smiles.

Fortunately we both spoke American English. We went to Bob's apartment, spoke more, and caressed. Then planned to meet the next evening. We enjoyed being with one another. Soon we alternated spending nights at each other's apartments. Some weeks later, Bob went to visit friends in Puerto Rico.

During this separation we planned to decide whether or not to commit our lives to one another or become only friends. When we met again, I am fortunate that Bob spoke first. I had decided not to commit. He had decided to commit. When I heard his decision, I lied to him, saying I had made the same decision. Only years later did I confess.

BOB

I was back at my apartment early on the evening of June 16, 1978. I had a dinner date with a young man I had met a month earlier. To kill some time I decided to stop by a gay bar, something I almost never did. After a while I noticed an attractive young man who seemed to be with a group of people. He was eating popcorn out of a brandy snifter. After a while I joined him. We ended up walking back to my apartment. I found it rather awkward telling him I had a date that evening. Could we meet again another evening? I was surprised when he said yes.

Joël and I saw each other throughout the summer. I began to wonder if this might go somewhere. That summer I spent many an hour walking about considering the possibility of another relationship. Would he want to? His personality was not the easiest I'd encountered. Would I have the patience to put the necessary work into this relationship? Toward the end of the summer, we decided to discuss whether or not to continue. We decided to continue.

JOËL

There seems to be some truth that opposites attract. When Bob and I started sharing our lives, we were certainly opposites. At the time, I was chatty, impulsive, idealistic, domineering, impatient, and angry, refusing to suffer fools (I am not too different now). Bob was often too quiet (was he hearing what I was saying to him?), indifferent to my passionate and fiery tangents, and at times he was not serious.

I was physically passionate, could not help hugging and touching Bob at every opportunity, wanted to be with him every second, and was eager to please. He was a good listener, could tolerate my tantrums and disappointments, was a creative cook, understood what made me tick, loved my attention, and made me laugh.

We also had many common interests. In addition to being newly in lust with one another, we had similar interests: especially things Italian, travel, food, music, learning, and felines.

It is important to emphasize how difficult it was to persevere during our first years together. Too many times I disliked Philadelphia or saw career opportunities elsewhere. I would deceive myself that Bob was not *the* right person for me. I was often jealous of Bob's friends and his need for independence.

The years teach us that in living, one thing we can count on is change. We remain different. But we have also changed. We have learned to respect our differences and to share our similarities as well as our possessions. Basically we remain the same individuals described above. Some qualities once in the forefront have receded. Others have come to the forefront. As a result of sharing our lives for these many years, we have learned to recognize and nurture the values that cause our relationship to flourish. Our success is the result of time and perseverance.

BOB

Although Joël and I had a lot of interests in common, our early years seemed to concentrate on our differences. I tend to be rather laconic, so Joël's volatility was often a help in lighting some fire under me. In fact, this was one of the conscious attractions for me. He helped me to get excited about things; on my own this rarely happened.

On the other hand, his volatility could be a cause for anxiety. I had encountered a similar personality before, my mother. I had learned to deal with this quite well, in fact my mother and I were very close. However, I knew it would take time and energy. Also, it took me a while to recognize that Joël perceived my calmness as though I were saying, "This is the way you ought to behave." I really did not want him to change. I loved him as he was. This is perhaps the trickiest part of a relationship. It is important to compromise, but vitally important that each person remain himself.

This difference in temperament obviously produced some conflict. How do you get anywhere when one person in the relationship reacts to anger by exploding while the other person clams up? We found something that worked for us. When difficulties arose we would set aside time each week to discuss them. Often this took the form of a weekly Saturday morning give-and-take. We would do this regularly for months, and then months went by without feeling any need for it. We have not abandoned this process and have no intention to.

J O Ë L

As Bob writes, open dialogue is an important practice for maintaining our relationship. We discuss in depth any problems we have with one another, with our jobs, families, or friends. Originally some topics were difficult to broach. With time, honest discourse has become easier. It keeps you in clear touch with one another. It is sharing.

Our views of religion, our backgrounds, and many of our interests differ. But we enjoy sharing many things and experiences. We travel together, read many of the same books, eat together nightly (don't tell anyone that Bob is the better cook), and volunteer for AIDS causes.

We met before AIDS and agreed not to discuss any flings. Since the foundation of our relationship is trust and occasional flings began to undermine this trust, we opted for monogamy. It happened just about the time AIDS appeared.

We often make love. I believed what society taught me: that gay men cannot have lasting relationships and that since we are promiscuous, we quickly lose interest in the sexual object at hand. Truth to tell, we are more in love and lust than ever.

While we do a great deal together, we also respect one another's independence. I have visited relatives in France, gone to professional meetings, and do many other things alone. So does Bob. Time apart is important. In the same vein, it is important to have one's own space at home. From time to time, you simply need to be alone.

BOB

As Joël just summarized, trust develops by enjoying our lives together while respecting and learning from our differences. It is important to recognize that differences will always be present, that one is not striving for some sort of homogeneous bliss, but the simple and wonderful sharing of one another's lives.

When differences do arise I find it helpful to ask myself, "How would Joël handle this without me?" I find that if I can remove myself as much as possible and also live with his decision, things usually work out. If he asks for my opinion I give it, but otherwise I try to keep my mouth shut. Sometimes it is not easy. One of the most difficult occasions was when Joël had decided on a change of profession. I felt strongly that it was a mistake and was very tempted to say so. Yet I also knew how much he wanted to make the change. I kept my mouth shut. He did make the change and found it not to his liking. I did all I could to help him return to his previous job. He has done the same for me many times. One key principle we observe is never to say "I told you so" or better yet, never to get into a position where we are tempted to say it.

We have talked a lot about how we interact and do things together. It is important to state, however, that remaining yourself means that some things must remain private. This could mean simply having some time to yourself or could mean questions of deep religious or philosophical significance. This has taken us time to work out and quite honestly develops from the fact that we have learned we cannot do everything together and need our alone-time.

JOËL AND BOB

Over three years ago, Bob stopped to help two cyclists fix a flat tire. His reward was a shot in the neck, the two racing away, leaving Bob to die. Joël walked into the hospital as if he knew what he was doing, handed the power-of-attorney document and a copy of Bob's living will to the hospital authorities, and began making the necessary decisions.

Joël was able to accomplish these tasks because we had our legal house in order. Because the government refuses to recognize our relationship, this is very important. If you own a house jointly, check with a lawyer where you live to put the deed in your names with right of survivorship. This ensures that no designing relative can take the property from the survivor. Get your lawyer to set up a durable power of attorney. Make certain you have a will,

no matter how young you are and no matter how little you may have. Some couples also need a contract spelling out who owns what. We never have.

For us Bob's shooting was trial by fire. One can never prepare for the changes forced by such an event. Bob had to give up his independence, was fed through a tube, could not talk or swallow, and we faced the possibility that this condition would last his lifetime. Joël had to continue working and, at the same time, had to coordinate with a veritable army of hospital, home health care, and HMO contacts, to say nothing of keeping in touch with family, friends, and well-wishers. Bob's two sisters and niece came to live with us for three months. Mary Jo Melberger, priest at Bob's church, helped us with so many practical and spiritual matters. We wonder what we would have done without them. Little by little, Bob recovered. We pulled out of this horror loving one another more than ever.

Change continues. Trials and tribulations, daily living, and the many good things have made us love one another more than ever. We do not know what the future holds. Who does? But we talk about it, plan for it, and look forward to living and loving into it together.

Howard Frey
and Walter Holland

-thirteen-

holding tight to our love

WALTER HOLLAND

Ten years ago I used to go to a gym on the Upper West Side of Manhattan. It was very eighties, very gay and splashy. Trainers tended to talk more about auditions for soaps and singing coaches than muscles and weights. Glass mirrors were everywhere to reflect back the various states of physique and endowment.

I would see Howard lifting weights on the Nautilus machine. He was short but strong-looking, compact and lean with a face reminiscent of Jean Paul Belmondo in *Breathless*, a film I rather admired. It was a Gallic face or perhaps Middle Eastern. He always appeared serious and his body, sturdy and tight, seemed to reflect a steady discipline. For weeks I would encounter him, always at the same hour, always at the same machine. I would be on the treadmill, which afforded me a view of his usual spot and position. In the beginning we barely made eye contact, a furtive glance, a quick aside. At first, I didn't understand his attraction to me, given the surfeit of gym boys strolling around the training floor. I later surmised that a certain insecurity, a nervousness about his social prowess as opposed to his physical appearance, had steered him toward my more nonthreatening manner. After a few weeks, it became a heated pursuit, a thing of fantasy as I tried to guess his profession and various preferences. Week after week I would stare at him, sometimes with varied response.

At that time I was sharing a West Side apartment with a gay roommate who was an editor at St. Martin's Press. My editor roommate and I frequently talked boyfriends. We were both single. I had gone through a round of assorted relationships: the hot, sexually compulsive, and totally unreliable actor; the bisexual college professor; the Mexican doctor working as a waiter illegally; the German doctor who was a frequent patron of gay baths; the movie-theater-manager-puppeteer who had just turned HIV positive; the poet who was breaking up with a lover of several months; and the most recent, a psychologist who manipulated me to obsessive lengths. The psychologist also had an incredible sexual charisma that I couldn't quite evade.

It was my belief, then at the age of thirty-two, that I had no hope for a long-term relationship with another man. My editor roommate would come home at night from a long dinner conference or a stuffy East Side party drunk on Scotch and pour out his fears and insecurities. AIDS was becoming a reality, and I was steadily afraid of contracting the strange and deadly disease. Friends were dying. I saw my former lover, the bisexual professor, as representative of the split, frenetic life I was heading toward, a life of furtive, quick relationships. I had no confidence in myself. I was still on-again, off-again with my psychologist friend. I would call him up, get his phone machine, and ask him to dinner or a movie. I never knew if he would reply to my messages. Sometimes he would call me at midnight and have phone sex, then three weeks could go by without a word. It took him months before he would invite me to his apartment, and the only night he ever asked me to sleep over until morning was the night I left him for good.

One Saturday, completely despondent, I ended up at the gym. I saw my "friend" on his usual machine. We did our series of glances and finally, totally spontaneously, I found myself walking toward him. I had no idea what I would say. The only thing that occurred to me was that I had been thinking of getting my own apartment, so, stepping up to him, I smiled and politely asked if he knew of any apartments available for rent on the Upper West Side. This opening line seemed totally plausible at the time, but in retrospect, several minutes later, as he was stumbling to give me a few distant leads, it seemed horribly stupid. He was cordial, and toward the end of his speech, he suggested that I come over and inspect his apartment and building as it might give me some ideas. I accepted but only on condition that afterwards we would go out for dinner.

An hour later I found myself inspecting his one-bedroom apartment with terrace overlooking Amsterdam Avenue. Then we went to a tiny Indian restaurant in the neighborhood. Our waiter was an unusually flamboyant gay man named Michael from the state of Georgia (who we would come to know over the next several years through frequent visits to the restaurant). Michael kept us entertained with his wry sense of humor and his stories about his various cultural close encounters with the Indian staff at the restaurant. Dinner involved the usual date chatter: jobs, living arrangements, and education. At the end of the meal, however, I discovered that I had failed to take my wallet to the gym. I was totally penniless. I had no idea what to say or do. Red in the face, I announced to Howard that I couldn't pay for my share of the meal. He looked at me with a moment's displeasure and I sensed he might have seen it as part of some deception. I became all smiles and apology. I made him swear that he would let me take him to dinner the following night and to see his place again.

When I showed up at his apartment the next evening I think he was both surprised and relieved. I tried to be as punctual as possible. He let me in, played some music, and we talked while seated on his couch. He shared with me an interesting story. It turns out that at the gym I apparently had a double. This other gym-goer who bore a close resemblance to me would appear during weekdays, never on the same nights that I attended the gym. Apparently my double was decidedly not gay and decidedly not interested in Howard. This coincidence had led to all sorts of strange and confusing episodes: one day Howard's cruising asides were met with a curious, attentive smile, the next day they were totally ignored.

That was the first of several evenings with Howard. Cordial, polite, I would leave him after a few drinks and some music. I had decided to go slow, as my past had been full of hasty, dead-end affairs. Later Howard confided to me that his insecurities seemed to increase with these rather cool initial meetings. Sex was a validation of self-worth for him. He was used to instant sex. Indeed, a lot of his relationships had consisted in being used for sex and sex alone. During this first month of dating, we both continued outside affairs that were unfulfilling.

What struck me immediately as different with Howard was his great reliability and trustworthy nature. Phone calls were returned. A date was kept. I could actually plan my life and know that he would be there. He was a runner, and I learned to work around his exercise schedule. I was also pleased with his self-reliance and financial independence. He rented his own apartment. He had bought his own furniture. He had a good rapport with his parents, who accepted his gayness (he worked in his father's store at the time). I felt secure whenever I went to his apartment. I felt like his place was a home. There were no big dramas, theatrics. All the endless complications that other gay relationships had presented just fell away. He also seemed anxious to travel (something he'd already done a fair amount of) and had a routine life more structured than my own. An aspiring writer as well as a physical therapist, I had spent several years in limbo, dashing off poems, writing all weekend late into the night—emotional, depressed, frantically social, or withdrawn.

I was also frightened by the legacy of family dynamics (depression, aloof father), but at the same time, no divorces, all my siblings almost married. After a month I approached the issue of sex. I had worried about the chemistry between us. I was convinced that if there were an emotional bond, the sex would prove unsatisfying (a strange paradox I had come to believe in from previous experience and hearsay). On the other hand, sex was not so much an issue for me. What I really wanted was emotional stability. Howard had no confidence in his ability to attract someone beyond the physical. He eventually saw in my reticence about sex with him a new emphasis on emotional bonding, sensitivity, and friendship.

It took us months after we first slept together to strike a compromise between the rather rough, physical sex he had come to expect—almost mechanical and perfunctory—and the sensual, slow, and emotionally connected sex that I really desired. Before a year was out we decided to travel together as a great test of our compatibility and as possible preparation for moving in together (he was considering buying a co-op apartment). The trip to Germany and Italy proved to be one of my best, although I had failed to tell Howard of my fear of flying. It was only the day before that I confessed to my extreme anxiety. He became afraid that I would not show up for the flight, a fear which was heightened by the fact that a few hours before we were to leave I had retreated to the gym in the hopes of physically exhausting myself on the treadmill so that I would sleep most of the way.

We returned from Europe and decided to move in with each other. We had a house-warming nuptial party of sorts. All our then friends came over to peruse the empty new apartment. In the heat of that summer we took possession of our new home.

The real irony of our meeting and moving in with one another was that as a boy I used to visit my uncle in New York City. My uncle was an actor, and for years he was a customer at the camera store that was owned and operated by Howard's father. With time he had become friendly with Lou, Howard's dad, and also with Howard, who worked as a delivery boy. When I finally came out to my uncle and told him about Howard, my uncle's look of shock was more in response to the odd coincidence that I should be involved with Lou's son. "Nice people," my uncle said. "Nice people."

I've often wondered what it would have been like if my uncle had brought me into that store years ago when I was a gawky adolescent from Virginia hanging on to my playbill from the movie *Lawrence of Arabia*. As it was, he never took me there, but it seemed like the relationship was destined from the start. For his part, Howard had not associated my uncle's last name with my own. It was only when I described my uncle later that the connection clicked.

The years brought travel and more travel and a series of enormous losses for Howard and me. I lost five friends to AIDS. He lost several as well. His dad's store eventually went bankrupt, and I was forced to support Howard for a short time. I encouraged him to go to school, and he received an M.B.A. The degree led to a new career and a new job.

I grew to accept myself and to accept him, and I came to embrace a sense of security, place, and presence I had not thought possible being gay. Just when I wasn't looking for it, a mutually exclusive gay relationship materialized. Perhaps it has been subconsciously modeled on my middle-class family upbringing, the continuation of monogamous relationships, but I seem to find that approach personally more satisfying.

Strangers always marvel at the length of our relationship, they question it with great curiosity, but it still feels like yesterday that I was the nervous young man approaching Howard on the training floor. There are still insecurities and what-ifs, but the relationship has taken on a sturdiness all its own, a sturdiness which reminds me of him and those first few times that I felt him in my arms. It is something that gives me great strength and from which I feel a capacity for great compassion.

We now think alike. Occasionally I will rush home loaded down with dinner groceries only to find that he has preceded me to our favorite store by only a few minutes and has stocked up on the same familiar treats down to similar brands of wine. When I am out of town I know he will order duck from the Chinese restaurant and spend most of the evening with a bad stomach, just as I can never resist a dessert at a restaurant or café. I know that when traveling I will always be the one left in charge of directions and dealing with the map, and he will be the one to negotiate the hotel bill or carry the keys. We read each other's moods. I know when it is time to suggest a cocktail in our room to take the edge off a full day of sightseeing which I have instigated, and he knows when it is wise to keep quiet about sudden changes in the itinerary or photographic detours. He knows that I will always bring up the issue of buying a house or settling down in some foreign clime, just as I know he will obsess about his job on our trip and come down with a case of constipation.

We end each other's sentences and communicate in a subtle body language only we can decode. More than once, we have left the apartment only to realize that we are wearing similar shoes or shirts or the exact same color pants or jacket. Sometimes I have actually changed clothes because of this uneasy coincidence. In a restaurant the other day while sitting at the table I realized that we were matching bookends in terms of posture—both propped on one elbow, our bodies turned slightly to one side, heads at the exact same angle. I altered my position only to find that he matched me a few moments later.

We play to each other's strengths and weaknesses, so much so that I know he will handle the negotiations in some difficult business situation or crisis and I will handle them during the more subtle social occasions. He is quick to judge people and I am slower, but we always seem to intuit the same truth in human relations. He can be stony and silent as I often am, two isolated individuals poised at an invisible line that we dare not cross over, afraid to show affection in public or to family out of force of habit and conditioning.

He is always the first up in the morning, making the coffee, ironing the shirts, feeding the cats, and making noise. He always does the laundry and cooks, while I vacuum, dust, and clean up the dishes. He yells at the cab driver who overcharges while I try to draw a smile from the hotel clerk who has been irritated by his abrupt questions. He does not always see the beautiful spot or vista a few yards off or know how to locate this or that monument, but he's good at arranging train tickets in a pinch and keeping things to the budget.

I have attended both of his nieces' bat mitzvahs. His mother and father frequently took us out to dinner and talked politics. Knee-jerk liberals, the talk was always lively. My parents voted Republican and tended to revere the World War II generation of Reagan, Dole, and Bush. Howard's family loved the beach. From their early years, Howard's parents religiously would go for a weekend to Long Beach and stroll along the oceanside. Howard's resulting love of summer and the sea made us seek summer shares at Fire Island.

In the city, when Howard's parents would visit us, Howard and his dad would walk a block ahead while his mom and I would talk about Howard as a young boy and his similarities to his father. She would tell me amusing stories of his youth, and some of these incidents would explain his odd obsessions and curious tics. Reviewing the family photos I felt more drawn to the various sides of Howard's life: infancy, boyhood, manhood. I saw him as a lean adolescent with a long mane of hair standing next to his parents at Long Beach. I saw a quick shot of him as a teen on the harbor front at Mykonos and wandering through the streets of Rome with his sister. I saw a photo of him on a beach in Spain in his early thirties in a striped T-shirt looking carefree and sexy. While I went to noisy gatherings for Passover, he came down to Virginia for a traditional Christmas or Easter and listened to my mother talk about the D.A.R. While his parents would come to the gay beaches of Fire Island to peruse the pierced and tattooed sun-worshipers with amused curiosity, mine would meet us in Colonial Williamsburg and Norfolk for a visit to the azalea gardens. One of my biggest regrets was that my parents never met his.

The night before his mother died, we both went to her bedside and said goodbye. I accompanied him home on the train from Long Island. A week later we were at the old condo with his dad as he sat shiva. I rode in the family car with Howard, his dad, his sister, and her husband to the cemetery. Later, Howard and I walked with his dad one cold day along a beach in Long Island as his father cried aloud. Tears streaming down his face, we talked of her, the three of us, trying to reassure this suddenly frail and aged man that his life would go on. On the anniversary of her death, we went to the unveiling of her grave monument and spoke of our memories together.

We have seen friends die of AIDS. Howard's ex made the trek from California to Fire Island for one last summer in the sun. Thin and sickly, he sat on a deck in Cherry Grove and told me that he was happy Howard had found me, that Howard deserved happiness in this life. He made me promise to hold tight to our love.

Howard and I have marched together at demonstrations, walked down Constitution Avenue in Washington numerous times, been to memorial services, open-casket funerals, and small group encounters with grieving friends. We have seen friends lose lovers, break up, move far away, change their careers, and we have heard the whispered secrets and problems of co-workers, family, and dying friends.

On a recent trip to Greece, my sister came along with us. Both she and Howard compared notes and I realized how similar they were in age and temperament, more practical-minded and rooted than I have been. On a visit to my parents for the holidays, my mother for the first time hugged Howard in front of me. For Howard's birthday my father sent Howard a check for money, more money than he'd ever sent me on my birthday, and now once a year my dad gives both Howard and me a check, the same check he mails quietly to my sisters and their respective husbands.

On my own I sometimes hear Howard's inflection in my voice, the occasional hesitations and repetitive phrasings. I have watched the gray appear in his hair. I have watched his running speed gradually slow and seen how we both have aged, our faces and bodies filling out and maturing. We each know the balance to our routines, the harmonious blendings of work and play, sex and travel. Sex has grown better. Over the years we have shared afternoons in Fire Island, Portugal, Greece, and Italy languishing in bed, frisky Saturdays at home, and impromptu lovemaking after work.

Early dramas have been replaced by small and quiet rituals of mealtime, leisure time, walks, and shopping that seem to establish a beautiful rhythm that goes beyond words. We share friends, enjoy summers on Fire Island, and really lead very quiet lives. Sometimes on a street in a strange town or country we draw hostile stares, but we've never feared for our lives. We marvel at the naturalness and compatibility of our existence. He is still socially uncomfortable, at times has difficulty expressing himself verbally and publicly, and in his shyness presents a cool exterior; I am sometimes intellectual, obtuse, withdrawn, and prone to restlessness; but we never seem to run out of things to say to each other or to learn, even if he plays the practical half and I play at being romantic. Be it compromise or a choice to sometimes leave things unsaid, we know that there are limits and we know that there are dangers, but we respect each other and we can live among those differences.

Alden   Reimonenq

and   Darrick   Lackey

-fourteen-

fictive snapshots and twenty-three anniversaries

ALDEN REIMONENQ

Remembering how we marked the twenty-three yearly occasions of our relationship seems fictive to me as I collect and consider the mundane or sublime interactions that comprise our family history. Furthermore, through the very act of remembering, I realize I am remaking our history into our story. Pressed as I have been to capture our most memorable moments (from a treasury of celebrations, scandals, fights, infidelities, deaths, and many other joys and sorrows), those few that have burned brand-like into my memory are stories that reshape themselves constantly. Thus the few family snapshots shared here carry with them the spirit of our dense love, a love we have come to know as a mature pleasure.

Darrick DeWitt Lackey and I met at Purdue University in early October 1974. Darrick, from Gary, Indiana, was twenty and in his junior year as an undergraduate in the Krannert School of Business. I was from New Orleans, Louisiana, married, twenty-two, and in my first year of graduate school. While my wife searched for full-time employment, I worked on a Ph.D. program in English, held a fellowship, and taught two courses in freshman composition. That Darrick and I met at all was a near miracle considering the 38,000 students who then attended Purdue. We now realize that surely coincidence was our Cupid: Darrick took a Greek tragedy course, in Heavilon Hall 106, from the very same professor who taught my graduate Shakespeare course in the very same room an hour later. I had seen Darrick often and was attracted to the cut-off jeans that barely covered his ample behind and fully exposed his sexy bowed legs. His waistline was tiny, almost girl-like. All in all, there was something hauntingly masculine and alluring about him. He never gave me more than a nod of recognition in those early days, but he never shirked a "brother's" obligation to tender that nod. I read much more than black solidarity into his actions, hoping that one day we would do more than just nod. With that hope, I took to coming to Heavilon Hall before his class adjourned just to see him.

On several such occasions, I coaxed Darrick to go beyond his nodding by posing lame questions about our common professor's quirks or the subject of preferences for Aeschylus or Sophocles, but the real conversation came when finally I alluded to teaching writing. Darrick beamed with interest: "Maybe you could help me with my paper; it's due in a week," he asked in the sweetest sincerity. "I'm not very good at literary analysis, and this professor should only be teaching you graduate students. He acts like we're bothering him." The rush I felt at that moment comes back to me now. Without hesitation, I invited Darrick to dinner with the promise that we would work on his paper.

The beginning of that October in 1974 could not have been more picturesque in its array of autumnal color. The orange-red leaves of the elms made a luscious spread just in front of our apartment. My romantic bent tells me that this, my first experience with the change of seasons, signaled a deeper change in me. With the wish for a relationship with Darrick goading me on, I saw more clearly the patent unfairness and immorality of continuing my fictional heterosexual marriage. Guilt tugged relentlessly against my prayers for a satisfying male love match, but I played the husband in a production scripted for a very hurtful ending. During this time, I always waited in the window to gawk at Darrick's sexy loping across campus, blowing cigarette smoke furiously as he hurried to our door. Invariably, he ignored the sidewalk and disturbed the carpet of leaves as he would the blanketed snow later during winter's rage.

We worked on his paper as my wife watched television and ignored us after asking small-talk questions about Darrick's girlfriend. Darrick and I fell to our studies, often brushing arms then pulling quickly away, or staring into each other's eyes long enough to take notice then redirect our gazes onto our papers. Now we recognize these playful preludes as our first attempts at banter, but then we dared not give name, voice, or even recognition to the passion behind such tame movements. Yet such lusting could not simmer much longer, and it was Darrick who dared first to vent the heat.

The longevity of gay relationships is not generally measured by markers such as wedding dates; consequently, gay partners often have problems fixing dates for anniversaries. Tracing our anniversary date is easy, although our recollection of our first date conjures up different qualifiers: Darrick remembers it as "fantastic" while I label it "curious and weird." Nevertheless, the whole night was cast in high drama—drama fit for many an animated retelling.

"*Lady Sings the Blues* is playing at the Elliot Hall of Music on October 25. How about we double-date?" He asked this without the smile I yearned for; I wondered why he was so serious.

By this time, my wife and I were rehearsing our imminent estrangement, precipitated undoubtedly by my growing attraction to Darrick. To his invitation, I blurted, "Sure, but why can't we boys go alone? I deserve a night without being saddled to the Mrs." Darrick's charming smile, framed as it was by his full lips, returned. His smile was magnetic, so much so that I offered to walk him back to his dormitory to stretch out the pleasure he so effortlessly exuded. On our slow walk to Owen Hall, we planned our upcoming night out. This was also the first time I expressed my distaste for Darrick's smoking. He immediately hurled away his cigarette.

In front of Owen Hall, our privacy was interrupted by students constantly prancing in and out as if on a conveyor belt. We had not satisfied our need to talk, and Darrick's offer to walk me back to my apartment felt like a gift. For hours, we shuffled through the flame-colored leaves, yapping until our laughter pulled my wife out of bed and to the window, a clear sign that the night's rendezvous had to end. The anticipation of our first date on the weekend, however, was enough to sustain us. In those our most closeted days, we seduced each other feverishly by playing straight male roles to each other. The lie itself was an allurement.

I had always hissed that Diana Ross was hot as fish grease and should never be called a lady, but on October 25, 1974, I bit my tongue and fictionalized my enjoyment to match

Darrick's. What followed the wretched movie made enduring Miss Ross's screen riot worth the pain. Darrick had not acquired a "man's" taste in alcohol; he drank sloe-gin fizzes, and I was happy to accommodate him. After one fizz, my wife went happily to her slumber, leaving us to our boisterous laughter and exaggerated maleness. We watched television, sinking fizzes until we had to pry loose the last and most stubborn ice tray. Darrick volunteered to fix the next round, showing himself to be quite at home. But the gin fizzes and unyielding ice tray presented too formidable a battle for him; he cried, "Hey, what kind of man does it take to get this thing loose?"

The gin had stirred arousal juices in me, and before Darrick could protest further, I was behind him, enveloping him as I dislodged the ice tray. Darrick turned to face me, and with my arms already positioned to embrace him, I kissed him. My fear that he would respond negatively was allayed when he exclaimed, "Wow!"

At 2:40 A.M., we immediately launched on a direct course to the privacy of my office in Heavilon Hall. The night's coolness did nothing to chill our fever. Our collective memories recall only movements: belt buckles hitting the floor; loose change jangling everywhere (some coins found only the next day); writhing and thrusting; mounting and dismounting; and sprays and sprays of wetness after seemingly endless frottage. It took less than a month to go from first meeting to first kiss and beyond. Yet from that night to this, I have never seconded the feelings of freedom I experienced captured as I was in Darrick's arms that first night. Unwittingly, our closets allowed us to stage a drama for each other with the very act of maleness that we had longed for in our imaginations. In this man's arms, I knew then, as I know now, how I would define love. Of the most permanent and revered moments of our history, we will always rank our first kiss, laced as it was with sloe-gin fizzes, as the most vivid, colorful, and holy.

After that night, the years stacked themselves behind us: past divorcing my wife, Darrick's finishing his B.A., my finishing an M.A. and Ph.D., Darrick's moving back to Indiana to work, my moving to Chicago to work and to be close to him, and most important, our pledging a life together. With the next six October 25s came quiet celebrations often passed with just a phone call commemorating our first date and continuing love. It was not until we moved to California that our anniversaries became annual celebrations, prized in parties, gifts, and lots of surprises.

My being transferred by AT&T from Chicago to Pacific Telephone and Telegraph in San Francisco was a major blessing. When I announced to my mother that I was being transferred, her first question was, "What about Darrick?" Although Darrick was out to his family, I was still too Catholic to come out to mine. What assumptions they made were theirs to own, but I did not exacerbate what was sure to be a problem in 1981. Although my family knew Darrick and I were very good friends, I always kept a girlfriend offstage to continue my closet management. Thus I answered, "Mama, Darrick has a very good job with Union Carbide in Gary; he's not going to quit that job to traipse off to California on some kind of adventure. Jobs are too hard . . ."

"I give him a month," she interrupted.

After only twenty-five days, Darrick moved into my condominium at 1830 Lake Shore Drive in Oakland and found a job in San Francisco. We bused ourselves to the city, and while the commute and daily grind energized Darrick, my work with Pacific Telephone soured almost as soon as I set up my office. Luckily, St. Mary's College hired me to teach Shakespeare and African American literature. It was there that I met a black administrator who introduced us to a network of black gay couples, many of whom had been together for decades. Becoming a part of this Oakland community of black gay male couples enriched our lives immeasurably. The ethos of the black gay scene in Chicago was primarily a singles' network with a burgeoning dating arena wherein folks recycled lovers seasonally. Darrick and I lived as outsiders in that community. In Oakland, we thrived having found nurturance, intellectual stimulation, and family-like support.

Moving to California meant scores of visitors from across the country: family, friends, friends of family, and unknown family all descended on us. On October 25, 1984, we were entertaining such guests when yet another family snapshot was framed. We had moved into the first house we bought together at 4717 Fairfax Avenue. Folks called it the "doll house" because it was small, resembling a Lake Tahoe cabin. We liked having company and enjoyed, most of all, taking folks on Bay Area tours.

On this our tenth anniversary, we were parading our Los Angeles friends Mike, Chris, and Ron (all since stolen from us by AIDS) across Fisherman's Wharf until late in the evening. Returning to the doll house, we found our machine chock-full of messages from well-wishers who all said about the same thing: "Call us as soon as you get in." That sounded usual enough, but after fifteen or so messages, I questioned what might be up. Before we had time to imagine anything, Jeff Potts, a dear friend, was ringing our doorbell, yelling, "Where have you cows been? Go get in my car right now."

We obeyed and found ourselves standing in Jeff's front doorway, holding each other as our friends shouted, "Surprise! Happy Anniversary!" Whenever we retell this story, we claim this as the very moment we felt married, for our friends had blessed our union and made us family. After endless rounds of Cooks champagne, we toasted our good fortune and wished for forever.

Our 1986 anniversary was dulled by a nagging escrow that foreshadowed a dark start to our lives in our newly built home at 3331 Wisconsin Street. One bottle of Cooks was all we had time to grab for celebration. Amid packing boxes, solving escrow problems, and praying our buyer for 4717 Fairfax would not dematerialize, we were too preoccupied for an anniversary party.

Our "daughter," Roderick Carter, however, against all refusals, came over, ass and face as usual, to kiss his "parents" congratulations. Rod was a dear boy who found his gayness at an early age and perfected it until his untimely submission to AIDS in 1994. His was a spirit full of all the happiness of uninhibited gayness and, sadly, full also of the angst generated by vicious loneliness. Rod was a major player in our lives, acting out many parts. When he pretended to be manly, it was hilarious because his very gait was "girl." We loved Rod as if he were our child. Folks often remarked that if it were possible for Darrick and me to have a child, Rod would be ours in looks (fair-skinned like me but with Negroid features like Darrick) and temperament (with my fire and Darrick's grace). Rod and I fought constantly; Darrick mediated constantly. I wanted Rod to settle with one lover, buy a house, and come to Sunday dinner as normal gay children do. Darrick wanted Rod to do what Rod eventually did: have several short-term husbandettes and buy a condominium (six blocks from us) in which to entertain them. Darrick's reasoning was that the heterosexual family model does not always work for us, so let's not force it. And so, on the occasion of our anniversary in 1986, Rod arrived just as Darrick proclaimed that he and his entire department had been fired from Crocker Bank. Clearly, I was in no mood for Rod's antics, especially not his saying, "Well, Dad, what are you going to do? Mom just got fired. Does this mean we aren't moving out of the flatlands to the hills? Stuck in ghetto life once again. I knew I should have found ugly, rich parents instead of cute, broke ones." Darrick laughed into a howl; I grimaced.

Darrick found work almost immediately after the house closed escrow, but moving into the new house was not without travail. The day we moved in, on November 1, 1986, rain was not predicted, but rain it did, in more ways than one. The mail brought a supplementary tax bill for $1,500.00. Soaked and exasperated, I sat on the front steps until Darrick coaxed me in. I stood in the doorway, clutching the bill, and with all the drama I could muster, I shouted in my best Scarlett O'Hara impersonation, "If we have to beg, borrow, cheat, steal, and kill, they are not going to take this house from us." Darrick, in an affected drawl, said simply, "Baby, ain't nobody gonna take Tara from us." Thus 3331 Wisconsin Street became Tara, host to New Year's Eve parties for five consecutive years, celebrating our debt, prosperity, and deep abiding love.

There is always residue from such awful beginnings, no matter how healing the outcome. Perhaps it is just my Southern upbringing, but I have always felt that we should have voided the house of whatever unchecked evil was lurking within. Several times I asked Darrick about having the house blessed. Some extenuation always prevented our doing so, and for that reason, I felt for a very long time that we couldn't shake a series of tragic and near-tragic events that plagued us during the early nineties.

During those years, death was a nagging cough we could not soothe. We tired of changing address books and going to memorial services. We suffered through survivors' guilt and the trepidation that someone very close to us would succumb to "the big disease with the little name." Worse still, we lived in complete denial over our coming down with the disease. Our denial was intense, if not pathological. We created a fiction—which we publicly pronounced often—that we were fine and did not need to use condoms because our relationship was monogamous. Secretly but separately, we had taken the HIV test, and because we were negative repeatedly, we lived the fiction that we did not have to worry. But worry we did. As we have confessed to each other since, the long incubation period shoved us into the ranks of folks who took the test every six months. We did not let on to each other that we believed we *should* be using condoms. That we both had taken side trips from our relationship had never been admitted; such posturing kept us walking just steps ahead of the shadows of our "outside" sex play. It all just seemed easier to manage through a mutual unvoiced code of denial. This all changed in 1994.

Darrick's stepfather, a gem of a man who accepted our relationship and treated me with enormous respect, died first that year, in the summer. There could not have been a clearer sky that evening as I waited outside for Darrick to come home. When I told him, I knew that the rest of the year was going to be troubled. Darrick reacted by repressing his feelings and holding fast to his resolve that he must get his mother through the crisis. I did not tell him that Rod had been ill until he returned from the funeral.

Throughout 1994, Rod was sick and unusually secretive, even with me. He never mentioned, even when it was obvious that he was dying, the disease's name in reference to himself. We enacted our parts in his fiction to help him cope with his impending death.

By September, my mother's health was failing. She was on kidney dialysis and had heart problems. Rod was in and out of the hospital, and we were in and out of his denial. When our anniversary came around in October, I was making plans to go home for Thanksgiving, so we agreed to have a small anniversary party at home. Rod came and was cheerful but gaunt and noticeably worried that others knew what his story was failing to hide. However, we all joked about his girlish waistline and avoided even the slightest mention of sickness or things medical. I remember distinctly the cynical grin Rod threw in my direction as I opened his gift. I commented on the sissy bow and prissy ribbon that made the gift stand out among the others. I said this, of course, to incite Rod to read me as was his vexing habit in healthier days. Through our gay language of knowing glances and smiles, we all imagined the lashing I would get for picking on Rod; we laughed just the same. He seemed to enjoy this, and as I went to kiss him to thank him for the gift, he held me close and said simply, "Bitch!"

I want to remember that night as happy, full of gay laughter and gay family sounds resonating with the fulfillment that freedom from our closets brings. I want to interpret the snapshot, capturing the moment as one in which we are all pictured with souls full of only the best thoughts for one another. And mostly, I want to imagine all of us embracing the life in us, a joyous life that can be kept alive through just the remembering. Yet I am unsure that the scene was just that way. Does it really matter?

By the end of November, we had buried my mother in Louisiana and Rod in California. And if Tara's cloud was not looming large enough, our beagle, Feste, died at age fourteen, just before Christmas.

The snapshot of Feste is remarkably distinct among all those we dote on. Never has a dog demanded that he be valued as highly as this dog. Feste, named after the wise fool in Shakespeare's *Twelfth Night,* was Darrick's Christmas present to me in 1982. We were living in an immaculate Lake Shore condominium with pristine white woolen carpeting, exquisitely appointed, and furnished far beyond our budget's capacity. When I came home Christmas Eve and discovered Feste, dapper with his huge red bow, he was taking the most fluid and generous piss in the dead center of the living room. I exclaimed simply, "Whose dog is that?"

I am truly grateful that love is infinite because Feste tested that notion daily. House training a beagle, an instinctual hunter and roamer, in a two-bedroom apartment was just the motivation we needed to buy a house—just to have the yard! After Feste shredded draperies, gnawed cabinet doors, and chewed clay pots, we put a down payment on the doll house, where he found a yard to hunt and protect. Feste's death hurt us tremendously because his colorful life linked us to the three most significant homes of our married life.

My mother and Rod were also anchors in our marriage, anchors that grounded us in a place that kept our souls fused and vibrant. Their passing let loose something solid between us that we are just now, in 1997, putting back into place. Since 1994, we have suffered through two major breakups and reconciliations. Something had to be exorcised from Tara, our bedroom, and our spirits in order for us to be whole again. Living every day and not being able to love in all the ways we were accustomed to forced us away from each other. We thought that what was missing was some deep feeling, the romance, or even the sexual spark. We found out, however, after grueling psychotherapy sessions, that we are still committed to our first sloe-gin kiss and all the storied snapshots that followed. Suffering the onslaught of huge and heavy losses wedged a space between us into which settled far too many chameleon-like demons.

As I write this, on the eve of our twenty-third anniversary, Darrick is asleep in our four-poster bed, with Ms. LuLu, our baby beagle, at his feet. When I stole into our bedroom to take off his glasses and slip away the AIDS fund-raising book from his chest, I discovered a greeting card on my nightstand. He had also set out my nightshirt and slippers. I kissed Darrick and Ms. LuLu and felt ecstatic until I turned to click off the lamp. It was then I saw that he had completely repositioned all the framed photos atop the television. I, of course, had previously rearranged Darrick's original arrangement. I smiled, admitting my defeat and remembering his toast on the occasion of our twentieth anniversary: "You're going to spend the rest of your life undoing everything I've done, but I sure love you."

Back in the cocoon of my study, I face my computer and this, our story. I find boundless comfort in our learning to respect the vast differences painted into the complex tableau of this difficult male-male love we barely understand. We will sleep better buttressed by the hope that the future will bring more of the gentle peace we have tonight.